THE
ASIAN GRILL

THE ASIAN GRILL

by CORINNE TRANG

GREAT RECIPES,
BOLD FLAVORS

CHRONICLE BOOKS
SAN FRANCISCO

Library of Congress Cataloging-in-Publication Data available.

ISBN-10: 0-8118-4631-8
ISBN-13: 978-0-8118-4631-8

Manufactured in Hong Kong

Designed by Joanne Lee
Typeset in Scala Sans, Landry Gothic, and Atma Serif
Cover photo prop styling by Spork
Cover photo food styling by Pouke

Distributed in Canada by Raincoast Books
9050 Shaughnessy Street
Vancouver, British Columbia V6P 6E5

10 9 8 7 6 5 4 3

Chronicle Books LLC
680 Second Street
San Francisco, California 94107
www.chroniclebooks.com

Weber, the kettle configuration, the kettle silhouette, and the
Ranch are registered trademarks of Weber-Stephen Products
Co.: Used with permission.

For Michael and Colette: You are my world
Astérix: You are one darling, patient pup

ACKNOWLEDGMENTS

Writing this book has been an interesting journey, one that I could not have made without a few key people:

Michael McDonough, I love you. Thank you for being my reader, my architect; thank you for asking the tough questions, and for pushing me to explore my work more fully.

Angela Miller, you are the best agent anyone could ask for. And yes, I'm already thinking of my next book project. Bill LeBlond, thank you and Chronicle Books for believing in this project and for your guidance.

For the country crew that persevered through overcast photo shoots and torrential summer rains: Jonadine Cheng, thank you for the recipe testing and food styling. Thank you, David and Mary Vidal; your ongoing support, kitchen, deck, wine cellar, and friendship were inestimably good during this project. Bruce Duffy, all I know about wood fires I owe to you; thank you. Thank you, Nancy Greenwald at the Arbor Bed and Breakfast in High Falls, New York, for sharing your kitchen and indulging my culinary flights of fancy. Suzen O'Rourke, thank you for your friendship, support, and the use of your test kitchen at Cooking By The Book in New York.

I thank Weber for their participation. I will always cherish grilling with not one but three Weber grills: the portable Joes on the fire escape, the vast Ranch Kettle on the porch in the country, and the gas-fired Summit. This book would not have been possible without these wonderful tools.

Thank you, also, Bruce Schimmel, Kate Maskar, Kimberly Kramer, Mickael Paradis, and Sooninah Gonsalves, for additional testing and tasting.

Thank you, Rick Smilow at the Institute of Culinary Education in New York, for giving me a platform for teaching the foods of Asia to an enthusiastic audience. Many thanks also to Mimi Martin at New York University for giving me the opportunity to teach food communications and journalism. As it turns out I love to cook and tell stories about cooking, too. And thank you Drexel University for our ongoing relationship.

I must also thank Anna Luerssen, Hayley Rosen, Sara Stracey, Shea Keating, Lacey Price, Marissa Maier, Sara Bylund, and Marilyn Villamar, for looking after Colette and making sure she always had fun, intelligent, and loving companionship. Thanks for throwing squeaky toys for Astérix to fetch, too. Thank you all, family and friends, here and abroad, for putting up with my endless absences and my lack of communication, and for giving me the time I needed to bring this book to fruition. In particular, I want to thank the most patient person I know, my grandmother, Jeanne Barbet. There is not one day that goes by when I do not think about you. Wait for me; I'm on the next flight to the beautiful Loire with Colette and Michael.

CONTENTS

INTRODUCTION: EAST MEETS EAST

Grilling is the perfect way to cook with Asian ingredients, especially if you like to experiment with new flavor combinations. Anyone who can grill in the standard way—a bit of marinade, a favorite ingredient, and a heat source—needs only a few simple guidelines to get started.

This book comes from years of conversations with friends and family, students and chefs, all of whom encouraged me to share my belief that virtually anyone who can grill a burger, chicken, fish, or vegetable is more than halfway to success with Asian grilling. The key is the marinade: marinades impart flavors. And if you can combine ketchup and hot sauce, you are ready to make marinades that include lemongrass, star anise, Thai basil, coriander, kaffir lime leaves, ginger, or galangal.

Most importantly, I wanted the book to be fun, to be a pathway to culinary adventure. As the daughter of a Chinese father and French mother, who was raised in kitchens throughout Asia and France, over the years I have developed a true passion for food. As a student of the complexity and longevity of cooking in the East and the dynamism and willingness to simplify and experiment in the West, I have traveled extensively, studying and cooking the cuisines of Asia through Western eyes. Through these experiences, I have developed a sense of what foods can combine successfully. The stalls in the night markets of Chiang Mai, Thailand; the refined, artistic kaiseki restaurants of Kyoto, Japan; and the side-street carts of Hanoi, Vietnam, all offer distinctive dishes that nonetheless hold certain principles in common. In these commonalities exists an approach to grilling that any cook can understand and use.

"East meets East" is the theme here, with grilling Asian style as the subtext: I guide the reader through the basics of classic Asian dishes and authentic herbs and spices (many of which can be found in local markets, and all of which can be mail-ordered), editing and adjusting so that everything is simple to prepare and will appeal to any palate. In essence, it is a culinary journey from teriyaki to tandoori and everything in between.

China is the great font, the grand beginning in all Asian cooking. Its culinary history is vast, encompassing over five thousand years, with more ingredients and dishes than any other place on earth. To grill Asian style successfully, however, you first need to master a few readily available ingredients, and then build as you go along. My soy sauce chicken, for example, is marinated in soy sauce, sugar, sesame oil, ginger, garlic, and scallions for 30 minutes (or up to 4 hours) before skewering, grilling, and serving. The ingredients balance the flavors of sweet and salty, bitter and spicy, and provide richness with a nutty overtone.

All Asian cuisines share basic cooking principles, and each brings something unique to the table. The notion that all meals have a starch as a background canvas and use protein and vegetables as enhancements is rooted in Chinese cooking, for example. From Southeast Asia come the French- and Chinese-influenced ingredients of Vietnamese cuisine (shallots, lemongrass, fish sauce, garlic), and the Indian-influenced ingredients of Thai cuisine (chilies, galangal, kaffir lime leaves, coconut oil); the extraordinary spices of India lie just beyond. East Asia as understood in Japan (miso, sea vegetables, sake) offers understated, clean flavors, and Korea (garlic, chives, chilies) provides bold and pungent tastes. The Philippines (garlic, onions, soy sauce) blend Spanish and Chinese traditions. And Indonesia (candlenuts, galangal, lemongrass, turmeric) offers the lessons of a great cultural crossroads.

All Asian cuisines are based on the idea that food and health are connected and that a varied and exciting—but structured—diet is the pathway to a healthy body and mind. The balance between different flavors, colors, and textures is traditionally expressed as the yin-yang principle. Ubiquitous in Asian culture, this principle is found in everything from styles of attire and architecture to floral arrangements, philosophy, and—inevitably—food. Here, it is expressed in simple-to-make menus consisting of one grilled food served alongside nongrilled but simple-to-prepare dishes. A refreshing mango salad and a steamed bowl of lotus leaf–wrapped herbal rice (ginger, garlic, and cilantro) with kaffir lime leaf–marinated pork skewers make a delicious, healthful meal that is balanced in texture, flavor, and color. It also typifies the yin-yang principle of food as preventative medicine.

First-time cooks of Asian foods will be surprised not only by the richness and variety of flavors available in these recipes, but by the unusual (to Western palates) blending of flavors. Asians make expert use of the five flavor notes—sweet, sour, salty, bitter, and spicy—at all meals and, in some cases, in each dish. For example, my grilled pork shoulder recipe mixes bitter and salty fermented black beans, sweet sugar, and spicy garlic. Menus are also rich in flavor notes, such as pepper-garlic hanger steak served with pineapple chutney and young leafy greens tossed in a sweet and sour miso-based salad dressing.

Another pleasant surprise is the relative lightness of Asian dishes. Chicken, pork, and seafood are common. And even beef, duck, and venison dishes can be light, because this richness of flavor will leave you satisfied with smaller portions. My miso-and-shiso-leaf-marinated sirloin steak or London broil, for example, can be served thinly sliced in small portions, along with raw zucchini salad and rice—another unforgettably flavorful meal with relatively few calories.

In general, my menus can be served like Western three-course meals with an appetizer, an entrée, and a dessert.

They can also be served in a more traditional Asian way by placing everything on the table at the same time, with fresh or grilled fruit in lieu of more elaborate desserts, which are generally eaten as an afternoon snack with tea.

Some dishes may seem familiar at first, but on closer examination they will surprise you. My barbecued pork is not the typical slow-cooked pulled pork of the Midwest and Southern United States, but one that holds together and stays juicy. The typical "barbecue seasonings" are replaced with exotic fermented bean curd, garlic, and rice wine. My wild salmon is modeled after the Japanese "maki" version, but not served raw as in many Japanese sushi restaurants. Instead, it is grilled and wrapped in sweet vinegar-seasoned rice, peppery fresh shiso, and clover sprouts, and then drizzled with a sweet lemon, ginger, and soy sauce dressing, giving it an explosive finish on the palate. My duck breast is spicy and savory, thanks to its Chinese five-spice powder, garlic, and fish sauce (or soy sauce) marinade.

I have also reinterpreted an American classic: the clambake. My version uses Asian aromatic herbs and spices with clams, lobsters, crabs, chicken legs, corn, and potatoes. Taking a note from Japan, dried kelp (kombu) is used as the seaweed base, bringing the flavors of the sea to the mix. The aromatics include lemongrass, galangal, scallions, kaffir lime leaves, and ginger. Serve this with a Vietnamese-inspired cabbage and carrot coleslaw for a refreshing note, along with Japanese-inspired rice pillows wrapped in golden tofu pockets.

A vegetarian menu also uses tofu, but as a grilled main-course dish. A Chinese-inspired dressing featuring soy sauce, sesame oil, ginger, and scallion enhances and deepens the nutty flavor of the tofu. (When tofu is correctly cooked it is not bland; it is rich, sweet, and nutty.) This dish is served with grilled bok choy and shiitake mushrooms, along with pickled carrot, daikon, cucumber, and cabbage, all served with plain jasmine rice for balance.

Fruits are eaten raw in Asia, often at the end of a meal, and are usually citrus types, to help digestion. Occasionally, they are cooked to intensify their flavor and render them more palatable. Fresh fruits can—due to poor weather, bad shipping practices, or any number of similar problems—lack flavor, palatable texture (be "mealy"), and natural sweetness. But mediocre supermarket bananas, mangos, pineapple, and peaches are markedly improved when grilled, as are pears and apples.

Grilled fruits can be a terrific addition to your menus, either as an unexpected accompaniment to pork dishes or as dessert. A mixed grilled-fruit dessert platter, for example, will delight your guests. If you want a more elaborate "Asian-themed" dessert, I have included a recipe for traditional Asian coconut tapioca soup, topped with grilled banana and toasted sesame seeds.

Exotic flavored drinks are wonderful starters for any meal, and I have included a litchi margarita cocktail and a watermelon mint julep, as well as refreshing nonalcoholic drinks like cucumber lemonade and a soy-based yerba maté (a mood-lifting South American concoction, reinterpreted here with an Asian flair).

A BALANCING ACT

Though based on a system of balances, Asian cooking lends itself to experimentation. Chinese cooking arts in particular draw on influences from as far west as Egypt and Persia. China is so vast that it combines mountainous regions, tropical and subtropical seas, deserts, arid plateaus, rich river valleys, and deltas—virtually every landscape imaginable. Famine has often ravaged the land, but trade with the known world ensured that an amazing diversity of ingredients would be present in the kitchen. China is so old that it is the likely source (or early adopter) of foods ranging from chicken to rice to countless fruits and vegetables.

This is the stuff of volumes of history and innumerable recipes. Suffice it to say, however, that both the novice and the experienced cook will find a few basic notions about Asian cuisine reassuring, because they are a way of making a vast array of ingredients more manageable. Notably, and uniquely in world cuisine, the Chinese emperor and the Chinese peasant dined according to exactly the same culinary rules; a starch, a protein, a vegetable; the five flavors; the yin-yang sense of balance in all things; and a range of preparation techniques, including grilling, braising, steaming, and stir-frying. If you follow my recipes and keep a few guidelines in mind as you branch out on your own, your food will taste better and you will be amazed at how quickly you will feel like a professional.

As in any evolved cuisine, the use of too many ingredients or too many similar kinds of ingredients at the same time can throw a meal out of balance. I have dined with three- and four-star French chefs who proudly mixed Asian ingredients into their dishes, generally making a mess of things. I once ordered a salad of young leafy greens with the "house dressing" at an upscale French restaurant in upstate New York. It looked so good when it arrived at the table that I could barely wait to dig in. Then the letdown: the chef had decided that sesame oil, soy sauce, black truffle juice, and olive oil could be mixed—but I can assure you, not pleasantly so. The chef did not understand that all these ingredients have the same intensity of flavor, and—like an orchestra trying to play four symphonies at the same time—the results were more than muddled. "Chef," I wanted to say, "you have now inadvertently created a too-many-flavors salad dressing. Instead, pick one flavor and build on it."

A beautiful sesame-oil-and-miso-based dressing of the sort made in Japanese restaurants, using sweet sake to counterbalance the salty and bold nutty flavor of the oil, with the addition of freshly grated pungent and mildly spicy daikon and young ginger, illustrates the principle of balance. As is sometimes true in architecture, less—when managed by a knowing cook—is more.

In a way, dishes like the "too-many-flavors salad dressing" also contributed to my passion for the ideas in this book.

I began to understand that, while East-meets-West fusion was promising, East-meets-East fusion offered much more dramatic results with a lot less effort. It was as if someone had said, "Here are five thousand years of food evolution stemming from a single source (China), amplified by innumerable national, regional, and local variations. Understand a few simple principles, and all this is yours for the taking."

I want to share my discovery with you: a virtual cornucopia of Asian flavors can be combined with the simplest techniques to produce meals unlike any you have tasted. It is as simple as a bit of marinade and a grilled steak. But the results can be as inspiring as filet mignon redolent with pungent garlic and licorice notes, and a sweet-citrus finish when dipped in a simple concoction of fresh lime juice, sugar, salt, and pepper. This is one of dozens of grill recipes in this book. Everything is explained in clear, easy, step-by-step instructions. Ingredient sources are included, and when appropriate, reasonable substitutions are suggested. The techniques will be familiar to anyone who has fired up an outdoor grill.

EAST MEETS EAST: MARVELOUSLY COMPLEX; PERFECTLY SIMPLE!

Some History

My father is very proud of his Chinese heritage and—having lived and worked in the food industry in both the East and the West—is something of a food expert. He particularly likes to recount bits of food history and is delighted when he can link ancient Asian practices to contemporary food trends. The recurrent theme here is: "China invented (fill in the blank)." On the subject of the grill he is—as he might say—"very correct."

Grilling seasoned food is nearly as old as human culture, and is often invoked as the first of many evolutionary steps leading to the cooking arts. The art is alive and well in the West, of course, part of the weekend cookout, the stove-top grill pan, and the restaurant experience. I have discovered,

however, that few Westerners realize the extraordinary importance of grilling in Asian cultures. Grilling meats, fish, fowl, vegetables, and fruits is part of the everyday Asian kitchen.

As a child, I observed my extended Asian family grilling indoors and out. And I continue the tradition, grilling most of the year, from early spring to late fall, and as long into winter as the weather allows. The beautiful floral, lemon, and licorice scents of Asian herbs intermingling with seafood, meat, and poultry as they hit the dry, fierce heat of a grill builds a sense of expectation. It is cooking, with a bit of theater (and aromatherapy) in the mix.

Grilling, like all heat cooking, most likely started through a series of serendipitous discoveries and happy accidents. Ancient Asians—like other primitive peoples throughout the world—lived off raw game for a part of their existence. They also found forest-fire-charred animals, and learned that these "direct heat" cooked meats had a different aspect. Meats lasted longer than the raw versions and tasted better than the burned, and the art of grilling was born. While modern Asia has highly evolved grilling techniques, we can observe the remnants of its earliest culinary discoveries on the steppes of northern Asia. There, the Mongols tend their nomadic fires as they did millennia ago, cooking meats over hot stones (and sometimes filling the cavities of animals with said stones). In this grilling tradition, simplicity was key. The nomadic Asian kitchen relied on basic foods directly connected to elemental fire, with few utensils and equipment light enough to be carried on horseback. Today's backyard grill (on wheels, perhaps) with skewers and a spatula is close to the mark.

Asia's northern nomads had little opportunity to cultivate crops, and they evolved distinctive regional grill traditions as a result. Relying on animals they could drive across grass ranges, in the hunter-gatherer tradition, they grabbed what they could while on the move. Spicing was basic beyond measure: often just a salt rub, an outgrowth of fundamental preservation and curing techniques rather than a quest for flavor. It is believed that the legendary ancient Mongols lived off the flesh of their dead animals as they rode on their far-flung conquests. Layered under their saddles, horse (and sometimes camel) meat was literally sweat-cured: salt-prepped on the run. Genghis Khan's armies would certainly understand the impulse behind the modern grill. Indeed, in Asian restaurants all over the world, Mongolian beef barbecue (a misnomer; it is grilled) is a dish still enjoyed much the same way it was on the ancient Gobi Desert.

Flavoring Techniques

Successful seasoning is sometimes still just salt, but more often salt artfully balanced with one or more spices or herbs. The most basic marinades have two flavor notes. The most complex will evoke the full five-flavors system discussed above. In the West, the salt flavor is most often from granulated crystals. In the East, it can be sea salt, rock salt, fish sauce, soy sauce, or a number of other more exotic foods, such as oyster sauce, fermented bean curd, miso, or shrimp paste. The sweet can be from honey or sugar, or—as often occurs in tropical Asia—coconut palm sugar. The spicy flavor can be as simple as ground pepper or as complex as Chinese five-spice powder. The bitter flavor can come from garlic, ginger, citrus zest, or wasabi. Finally, the sour flavor often comes from lemon or lime juice, rice vinegar, or tamarind pulp.

Beyond this, three flavoring techniques exist: dry rubs, spice pastes, and marinades. They are all used to enhance or alter the flavor of a main ingredient. A mild food, such as a simple chicken cutlet, can be intensified in flavor, for example, while gamey cuts of wild venison can be tamed and made more palatable. The pastes are particularly versatile, because they can be used as is or added to liquid-based marinades or dry rubs to form still richer pastes. The key concept is combinations of flavor: layers of subtle or assertive spices, herbal or fiery, as you see fit.

Dried ingredients—usually ground herbs, roots, leaves, and spices—are used to make dry rubs. While dry rubs can be used on virtually any food, they are particularly delicious on meats. (Fans of the famous Kansas City barbecue will recognize this technique.) Since dry rubs do not generally contain oil or other wet ingredients, the meat itself, with its natural juices and fat, provides lubrication as it marinates. As it cooks, the same juices and fats allow the dry rub to adhere. Dry rubs intensify the flavor of meat because they blend directly with the meat. A spicy dry rub might be brilliant on beef, for example, but overpowering on fish. For seafood or fowl, you might want to thin the dry rub out a bit, using the paste or liquid marinade techniques described below. A simple, popular, and readily available Asian dry rub is Chinese five-spice powder combined with salt and black pepper.

Spice pastes—like dry rubs—employ herbs, roots, leaves, spices, and a bit of liquid (oil or, occasionally, other pastes). Just a small amount of liquid is used, enough to form a clingy, condensed mass. Most of the moisture comes from the juices extracted from the herbs, roots, and leaves as you crush them. The small amount of oil moisturizes the mix and helps the herbs adhere to the meat. A typical basic Southeast Asian paste might include lemongrass, garlic, Thai chilies, galangal, ginger, turmeric powder, coriander seeds, palm sugar paste, and shrimp paste or fish sauce.

Marinades are herb-and-spice flavored mixtures in which all types of meats and seafood marinate prior to being cooked. Soy sauce, rice wine, sugar, pepper, and a bit of oil make a simple marinade, and herbs such as grated ginger and garlic, minced scallion and chilies enhance it. You can also add any herbal paste or dry rub to the liquid to deepen the flavor. The amount of liquid and the kind of food to be grilled are also important. While every cook will have his or her own preferences, when skewer grilling, I like to poke large pieces of meat with the skewer in several places, or cut it up into smaller cubes, with just enough marinade to coat the meat. I also turn the meat at various intervals to even out the marinating process and deliver consistent flavoring and moisture. There is no need to submerge the meat. Using more liquid will not intensify flavor (a common misconception). In other words, the marinade penetrates the food at the same rate, whether you use one-third cup or forty cups for one pound of meat!

Any cook hoping to master the art of the Asian grill will find the going remarkably easy. With a bit of fish sauce, sugar, and lemongrass, garlic, pepper, and oil, even a novice can be grilling an authentic five-flavor-note Vietnamese meal in a matter of minutes. These are the ingredients in the exotic-sounding and perfectly delicious *suon nuong xa,* or lemongrass pork skewers, a staple found at Saigon's (now HCM—Ho Chi Minh—City's) sidewalk food carts. And it gets simpler still. Some vendors sell from an impromptu grill: four bricks placed directly on the sidewalk, a small wood charcoal fire, and a grill on top. The cook squats in front of the apparatus, tending to the red-hot coals, arranging them in an even layer prior to grilling the meat, and calling out to customers as the herbal aromas waft on the evening breeze.

One of my most cherished memories of Asia's wonderful grilled foods is sitting at a midnight-bazaar food stall in Chiang Mai, Thailand. This northern region is (along with Bangkok) a major culinary capital of Thailand, and I have eaten many great meals there among the mountain peaks.

While my friends were off shopping to their heart's content at the indoor bazaar, it was the pungent aroma of herbs and spices in the outdoor air that drew me. I would walk up and down the food stall sidewalks. "The Grill Lady"—my nickname for her—caught my eye. She was plump, and all smiles. She noticed me (and my increasing curiosity), and pointed to the one empty stool left in front of her stall. Rubbing elbows with her customers (and my newfound Thai dining partners), I squeezed into place, determined to get my share.

I pointed to ingredients, she grilled, and I sampled. The skewered meats smelled good as they marinated, but when they hit the hot grill they sizzled, releasing the aromas of coconut milk, lemongrass, galangal, fish sauce, and palm sugar. That night I ate everything from beef, pork, and chicken to shrimp and squid. I sat there for over an hour, watching her turn the skewers frequently, crisping the edges but never burning the meats or seafood on her menu. It was one of the most memorable samplings of golden-brown grilled Thai satays and accompanying spicy peanut dipping sauce and refreshing, tangy and sweet cucumber salad I have ever eaten.

So here's to you, the grill ladies and gentlemen of backyards, picnics, seashores, and camping trips, of custom-configured built-in grills in urban lofts and fire escape mini-grills, of kettle-type drums on back porches, of oil barrels recycled as grills, of concrete-block improvised grills and fire pits and sticks.

Happy grilling—with all the flavors of Asia!

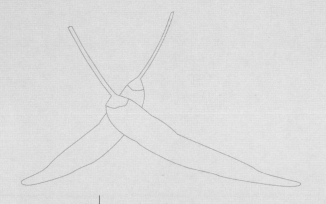

CHAPTER 1 | THE ASIAN PANTRY

Building an Asian pantry is a great way to get started with the recipes in this book. The idea here is simple: If you are going to the trouble of buying one or two special ingredients, step back and take a more unified approach to getting organized. This may be best accomplished in increments, and I have incorporated a two-prong method for building your staples and ingredients lists: "Basic Asian Pantry" and "Advanced Asian Pantry." Both are further subdivided into dried (or jarred and canned) and fresh ingredients. Notes on building your cooking skills as you build your pantry are included (one supports the other), as are notes on fresh versus dry ingredients and shelf life, as well as a glossary of ingredients.

GETTING STARTED

Starting a basic Asian pantry can be as easy as a trip to your local supermarket, where many popular Asian products, including soy sauce, curry powder, dark sesame oil, noodles, rice, and a number of other Asian condiments, are now readily available. Note that many recipes also use such basic Western pantry items as salt, pepper, all-purpose flour, vegetable oil, sugar, honey, onions, and garlic, as well as familiar meat, fruit, and vegetable ingredients. Natural foods stores, specialty markets, Asian ethnic markets, and mail-order sources will allow you to add authentic Asian condiments and other foods to your pantry.

Learning how to grill with Asian ingredients is simple if you take it a step at a time. Remember, marinades are the key to great Asian-style grilling because they allow you to add flavor notes step-by-step.

Consider the various ways to build on a basic soy sauce–marinated chicken recipe, for example. As a first step, mix thin soy sauce with sugar or honey (to counterbalance the saltiness of the soy sauce), and marinate cut-up chicken parts in the mixture for 30 minutes to an hour. Not only will your grilled chicken have distinctive Asian flavor notes, you will have already touched on the ancient principle of balanced opposites, or yin-yang.

Add some grated fresh ginger to the sweetened soy sauce marinade for a spicy herbal note. A bit of sesame oil will bring a nutty flavor. Minced garlic adds a slightly bitter note. Cayenne pepper develops a spicy hot finishing note.

For the crème de la crème version of this soy sauce chicken, replace the cayenne pepper with seeded and minced Thai chilies, and add minced scallions. Now, add some rice wine in the form of Chinese Shaoxing wine or

sake (the Japanese equivalent) to round out all of the flavors. Now you've achieved authentic Asian cooking.

The soy sauce base for this recipe places it in the Chinese, Japanese, Korean, and East Asian tradition of cooking. Start with fish sauce instead, and you are on the way to creating a Southeast Asian dish recalling Vietnamese, Thai, or Indonesian (and so forth) cooking.

BUILDING YOUR ASIAN PANTRY

Cooking Asian style will be simplified if you build an Asian pantry as you learn. If you have most of the basic Western pantry ingredients mentioned in the first paragraph, you are already halfway there. The following items will augment your basics.

Basic Asian Pantry
(Dried, Jarred, or Canned Ingredients)

> *Cayenne pepper*
> *Cornstarch*
> *Curry powder*
> *Dark sesame oil*
> *Hoisin sauce*
> *Honey*
> *Soy sauce (thin)*
> *White rice vinegar*

(Fresh Ingredients)

> *Cilantro*
> *Garlic*
> *Ginger*
> *Lemons*
> *Limes*
> *Scallions*
> *Shallots*

Advanced Asian Pantry

(Dried, Jarred, or Canned Ingredients)

Once familiar with the listed basic ingredients, build on them with the following items. These will give you a more advanced pantry, exploring Asia's exotic flavors and textures.

Chinese five-spice powder
Dried lotus leaves
Dried shiitake mushrooms
Dried shrimp
Fermented tofu
Fish sauce
Miso paste, white (shiro-miso)
Nori flakes
Nori sheets
Oyster sauce
Palm sugar
Pickled ginger
Rice vinegar (replaces Basic Pantry's white vinegar)
Rice wine (Chinese Shaoxing or Japanese sake)
Soy sauce (thick)
Tapioca starch

(Fresh Ingredients)

Banana leaves
Galangal
Kaffir lime leaves
Lemongrass
Shiso leaves
Tamarind pulp (or concentrate)
Thai basil
Thai chilies

From these lists and the recipes in this book you can build your pantry incrementally and selectively as you go. If recipes require red miso paste (aka-miso) or dried lotus leaves, for example, add them to your pantry when trying the recipes.

FRESH VS. DRIED OR PRESERVED INGREDIENTS

Dried ingredients are obviously easier to source and store, but they are not always the best choice. Fresh ingredients are often preferable, but they are not always easily available. Here, I cover many of the most important herbs and spices employed in this book, and explain which versions generally work best and which alternatives make for good second choices. Note that the more you work with Asian ingredients, the more you will intuitively understand their structure and flavor.

In general, fibrous items such as lemongrass, ginger, galangal, and banana leaves are superb when fresh, and perfectly acceptable when frozen. They all freeze and defrost with very little effort and little damage to the food. If they are unavailable in your area, or if you feel that you have to order them in large quantities to justify shipping charges, rest assured that the frozen version will not compromise your cooking.

When lemongrass is dried, it loses so much of its flavor that it is hardly worth the investment. When I find good fresh lemongrass I buy several stalks, wrap them individually in aluminum foil, and freeze them right away. They can be thawed fairly quickly. If you can't find fresh lemongrass, a lemon zest and lemon juice combination works well in a pinch.

Fresh ginger is required for marinades, and fortunately it is increasingly easy to find in American markets. Ground dried ginger or ginger powder is used for baking. Candied ginger is something altogether different.

Galangal is available fresh, frozen, dried, or in brine. Fresh and frozen are best but brined is a good third option. Dried galangal is okay in soups and broths, but not in marinades.

Banana leaves are used in only a few recipes in this book, basically as a "lid" for pit-roasted or slow-cooked or smoked items. Use large lotus leaves (doubling the quantity necessary for the recipe) as a substitute. Lotus leaves are sold dried and have to be rehydrated in water before use. If you find fresh or frozen banana leaves, purchase a good quantity.

In general, thin, leafy foods with a high water content, such as kaffir limes leaves, Thai basil, cilantro, and shiso leaves, are best when fresh. They may be used in marinades, soups, and stews in their frozen form, if chopped. Of all the leaves, kaffir lime leaves retain their texture and color best when frozen. You can buy them fresh and freeze what you don't need. They are also available dried, but though they retain much of their flavor when dried, frozen is a better alternative. Fresh Thai basil can be hard to come by, but it is readily available via mail order (see page 163). Thai basil freezes well if the leaves are washed and patted dry prior to freezing. Shiso leaves are a bit exotic, and unless you live near a Koreatown or Chinatown or other similar ethnic Asian area, mail order will probably be your best bet.

Cilantro is often readily available in bunches. On the off-chance it is a rarity where you shop, when you do find it, buy a bunch and freeze it, washing and patting it dry first. The flavor will be good, but, as with Thai basil and shiso leaves, the texture will be altered.

Fresh garlic is extremely common in Asian cooking. It is almost always readily available and is definitely preferable to powdered garlic.

SHELF LIFE

Obviously, no preserved foodstuff lasts forever. Less obviously, perhaps, many jarred, bottled, salted, and dried foods have a fairly limited shelf life. These include fish sauce, oil, rice, and dry spices, for example. A fresh bottle of fish sauce will have a beautiful amber color. As it ages, it turns progressively darker until it eventually looks like soy sauce and forms salt crystals at the bottom. (You can hear the salt rattling around if you shake the bottle.) Old fish sauce won't harm you (it is basically salt). It will be unrefined and overly salty, however, and its once-prized fish flavor will have dissipated beyond recognition. Southeast Asian foods

such as Thai, Vietnamese, Cambodian, and Laotian depend on the subtle fish note for their unique flavors, just as the foods of China, Japan, and Korea depend on soy sauce for their seasoning. Since fish flavor is what makes fish sauce interesting, old fish sauce is just about useless. Fish sauce can be refrigerated after opening, which will retard the aging process, but not stop it. Fish sauce is best up to 6 months after opening. Always buy condiments according to the amount consumed; that is, if you do not cook with fish sauce often, buy it in small quantity. The same goes for soy sauce, chili sauce, and so on.

Canned, powdered, and dried foods also have a limited shelf life. I once went to a friend's house and asked, "Do you have any curry powder?" After ferreting around in the back of her cabinet for a while, she proudly produced a can of the stuff. On opening it, I was surprised to find that the yellow powder had turned to near black. In the cupboard for several years, the powder had darkened and, its exotic herbal aroma now long gone, had taken on the taste of metal. The same person's dried shiitake mushrooms were several years old, and some had disintegrated into a fine powder. Her rice had bugs in it; her noodles were the same. No harm was done; we cleaned out the cabinets and started over with new ingredients. She had now come to realize, however, that canned, powdered, and dried did not mean "forever."

Storing Ingredients

When purchasing, always check the manufacturing and or packaging date of the ingredient.

Before storing the ingredient, date it with a permanent marker. *Note: Dried spices last about a year.*

Buy bottled, jarred, and dried ingredients in small quantities until you know how much you will use over a six- to twelve-month period. Once you have established a pattern of use, adjust the quantities you purchase.

Store dried ingredients in stainless-steel or ceramic jars, not in light-admitting clear glass. Place them in a cool, dark place. Bottled and jarred condiments should be stored in cool, dark places as well. Once opened, store them in the refrigerator. In the case of fish sauce, soy sauce, and similar products, refrigeration reduces the rate of fermentation.

Oils become rancid within three to four months. The best way to store opened oil is in a screw-top bottle. While they may seem convenient at the stove, stainless-steel oil canisters are not recommended for storing oils, because they are not airtight. (Once the oil is exposed to air, it starts going bad.) Use these or other decorative canisters only for dispensing, putting no more than a week's worth of cooking oil in them and replenishing the supply just as you need it. You should wash the canister once a week. Corked bottles are not airtight and are not great for storing, either. If your favorite oil comes in a corked bottle, simply transfer the oil to a screw-top bottle. Always store oils in a cool, dark place, like the pantry, or in the refrigerator. *Note: If you like using different types of oils (grapeseed oil is my favorite for cooking Eastern foods, olive oil for Western), buy them in small quantities.* Remember, once the bottle is opened, it is only a matter of time before the oil starts going rancid. Fresh is best!

Unless you cook for a very large family or large groups of people, buying bulk staples is not the best way to buy food. Buy twelve boxes of pasta or Asian noodles at a big-box store, for example, only if you plan on eating all of it at a big party or within six months. The same goes for all types of rice and flours, which also go stale.

A GLOSSARY OF ASIAN INGREDIENTS

When possible I have given brand names for some favorite store-bought ingredients, in parentheses.

Bamboo Leaves
Sold in Asian markets or from mail-order sources, dried bamboo leaves are long, narrow, and pointy at both ends. They should be soaked in water until pliable before wrapping foods. Bamboo leaves impart a slightly bitter flavor to rice and all sorts of food, especially when the food is allowed to cook for extended periods of time.

Carambola
Cultivated in Southeast Asia for centuries, the carambola is popularly known as star fruit because its longitudinal ribs (generally five) resemble a star when sliced. Unripe and lime green in color, it is used as a sour vegetable and can be added to salads. It can also be added to stir-fries or soups. The ripe yellow (slightly sweeter) version has a sweet floral scent and taste and is eaten as fruit. Store at room temperature to ripen, or refrigerate.

Caraway Seeds
Also referred to as nigella seeds, caraway seeds are actually the dried buds of a member of the parsley family. Similar in appearance to cumin, caraway has a flavor mildly reminiscent of anise. It is used in baking and cooking in many parts of Europe, Asia, and North America. In Indian cooking, caraway is often part of a spice mix or employed in braised dishes. Store in an airtight jar in a dark, cool place.

Cardamom
Sometimes referred to as the "grain of paradise," cardamom comes from India and has been used in cooking for millennia. It comes dried and can be purchased whole, meaning with pods intact, or decorticated, meaning as brown to black seeds, in which case it is generally powdered. I generally buy the green cardamom pods, and grind them just as I need them, preferring them to the store-bought powdered form. Store in an airtight jar in a dark, cool place.

Cassia
Similar to dried cinnamon but sweeter, dried cassia bark is a native of China. It is now widely grown in Asia, including in Thailand, Vietnam, and Indonesia. Unlike cinnamon quills (see page 20), cassia is sold as a thick, corky piece of bark that is dark brown in color. Buy chunks or sticks. Powder these only as you need cassia for a specific recipe. If you cannot find cassia, use cinnamon, cutting the quantity by a third to a half. Store in an airtight jar in a dark, cool place.

Chili Powder (Korean)

Deep red in color, as opposed to cayenne's orange color, this chili powder is sold in plastic bags in Japanese and Korean markets or by mail order. Korean peppers, when fresh, are bright red and large, about three times the size of Thai chilies. They are, however, most often used dried in powdered form, either coarse ground or fine. Also look for chili threads used as garnish. (Wang)

Cilantro

Used in Asian and Mexican foods, fresh coriander is most often called by its Spanish name, cilantro. Also known as Chinese parsley, in Asian cuisines it is used in soups, in dipping sauces, or as an edible garnish. Tender and bright green, cilantro leaves add an earthy, refreshing flavor to all sorts of foods. Refrigerate for up to 1 week, rolled up in a moist paper towel and placed in a plastic bag, leaving the end open to allow the herb to breathe.

Cinnamon

Similar to cassia (see page 19) in flavor, and native to Sri Lanka, cinnamon is now grown in many parts of Southeast Asia. Unlike corky cassia bark, cinnamon is in the form of very thin, orange, inner quills (fine bark curls). Both cassia bark and cinnamon quills are harvested (peeled) from a tree in the laurel family. Use cinnamon or cassia interchangeably, but be aware that cinnamon has a sharp flavor note in comparison to cassia's mild and sweet overtones. Store in an airtight jar in a dark, cool place.

Cloves

Very pungent, with sweet floral notes, cloves are generally used in small quantities in cooking. The spice is native to the Molucca Islands in Indonesia (the leading grower). Indonesia uses a tremendous amount of its crop in the production of clove-flavored cigarettes, and an insignificant amount for medicinal purposes; the remainder is exported. Cloves are popular in dry spice rubs. Store in an airtight jar in a dark, cool place.

Coconut Milk

Use unsweetened coconut milk for cooking, so that you have control over the sweetness or saltiness of your foods. Many brands are available, and some have more cream than others. For rich milk, shake the can to mix the cream and watery milk together. For light milk, open the can and scoop out the cream, which is generally solid in consistency and collected at the top (or buy coconut milk specified as light). The cream can be simmered over low heat, allowing the liquid to evaporate and leaving behind the oil, which is used in Thai, Indonesian, and Filipino cooking. The cream can also be added to coconut ice cream for a richer texture. You can make your own coconut milk by finely grating the meat of a mature coconut, adding 3 cups of boiling water to every cup of grated meat, and allowing it to sit for 1 to 2 hours. The difference between the milk and cream will be apparent, with the creamy part floating to the top. Canned coconut milk, however, is convenient and perfectly fine to use. There are plenty of good brands. (Thai Kitchen)

Coconut Vinegar

Made from coconut sap that is left to ferment for one to two months. Cloudy white to clear amber in color, it gives a light coconut flavor to salad dressings, dipping sauces, or marinades. It is less acidic than rice vinegar (see page 24), although the latter can be used as a substitute. (UFC Coco Vinegar)

Coriander Seeds

The seeds of the coriander plant. Like most dried spices, these are best bought whole and ground fresh. Coriander seeds are not as pungent as fresh coriander nor are they used in the same way. Coriander seeds can be added to braised dishes such as curries, or to dry rubs and spice pastes for a slight lemony flavor. For a deeper flavor, toast the seeds before using. Store in an airtight jar in a dark, cool place.

Cumin Seeds

Originating in Egypt, cumin is now grown in tropical climates including India, where the spice is used abundantly in curries and spice mixes for a slightly bittersweet aroma. Resembling caraway seeds (see page 19), they are oblong in shape and similar or lighter in color with nine long ridges. Store in an airtight jar in a dark, cool place.

Curry Paste

Made from a variety of fresh herbs and spices, such as galangal, lemongrass, kaffir lime peel, shallots, garlic, and shrimp paste, Thai curry paste (green, yellow, or red) is available in Asian markets or by mail order. A small amount will go a long way, as the Thai chili packs a lot of heat. (Mae Ploy)

Curry Powder

Made from dried herbs and spices, such as cinnamon, turmeric, fenugreek, coriander seeds, cumin, and green cardamom, curry powder is similar to the Indian garam masala, and they can be used interchangeably. Feel free to use Spice Route Blend (page 53) for Indian recipes requiring either curry powder or garam masala, as a dry rub for all sorts of meats and seafoods, or with tofu. Almost all spices and spice blends taste best when freshly made, so don't make more than you will need for a month. Store in an airtight jar in a cool, dark place.

Dried Lemons

Buy these in Middle Eastern markets or make your own: Buy a dozen or so whole lemons (or use leftovers) and lay them out on a baking sheet pan in a single layer. Let dry at room temperature for about 2 weeks until light in weight, an indication that all moisture has evaporated. These are so easy to make, they're not worth buying, and homemade dried whole lemons are much more fragrant than store-bought ones anyway. Dried lemons can be added whole to stocks, or powdered to add to spice blends. Store in an airtight jar in a cool, dark place.

Edamame

Lush green soybeans picked at the peak of ripeness (just before hardening), edamame are parboiled and frozen in their pods or shelled. The soybean in all of its manifestations has been part of the Asian diet for millennia. It is a great source of protein, and especially important in vegetarian diets. Edamame are crunchy in texture, and are often steamed and eaten as a snack. You can also add them to a tossed salad.

Fermented Bean Curd

Sold in glass or ceramic jars, and brined in rice wine, fermented bean curd (tofu) is a popular soy product used primarily in Chinese cooking as a seasoning. Cut into small cubes, it is tan in color, though it is sometimes made reddish through the addition of either red food coloring or red chilies. When in doubt, check the label. A small jar will go a long way, because each cube is extremely pungent and has a strong, earthy, fermented aroma. Once opened, store in the refrigerator for up to 6 months. (Pearl River)

Fermented Black Beans

These are oxidized soybeans that are salt-dried after being cooked. They should be soaked for about 30 minutes to get rid of excess salt prior to use in recipes. Some of the most delicious types have a subtle ginger flavor, due to the inclusion of the rhizome in the drying process. Fermented black beans are a Chinese specialty. They can be used in stir-fries, whole or chopped, and generally in combination with garlic, ginger, scallions, and rice wine. You can find jarred black bean and garlic sauce, but it is a rather poor substitute for the homemade version. Black beans are wonderful for creating interesting, slightly bitter, and salty marinades. Be sure to feel the beans through the plastic package. They should give a little and have a slight shine to them; this is an indication that they are moist. If they are dry, with white patches of salt, they are too old. Once the package is opened, wrap it in plastic and store it in the refrigerator for up to 1 year.

Fish Sauce

So many fish sauces are available at markets that choosing one can be a challenge. They range from mild to complex in flavor, and from salty to saltier. Made from anchovies layered with sea salt and stored in barrels in tropical temperatures, fish sauce takes over a year to ferment and is processed through several pressings. First-pressed fish sauce is the most expensive and is used for last-minute seasoning as a condiment at table. The second and third pressings, which are the types exported, are milder and are used in everyday cooking. Choose fish sauce that has a clear golden caramel color. The older it is, the darker it gets, and the less refined the taste. Buy fish sauce in small quantities and store it in the refrigerator for up to six months. (Phu Quoc, Oyster, or Squid)

Five-Spice Powder

The *five* in Chinese five-spice powder represents nature's five elements (water, metal, fire, earth, and wood), not the number of spices used in the powder, which can be as many as seven. The best five-spice powders come from China. Natural foods stores now sell their own versions, but they are mostly cinnamon-based, making them a poor substitute for the authentic version. If you have access to exotic Asian spices, you can make your own using equal parts dried cassia, star anise, fennel seeds, Szechuan peppercorns, cloves, ginger, and tangerine peel (see page 26).

Galangal

There are two types of galangal, greater and lesser. Greater galangal is native to Indonesia, whereas the lesser galangal (also known as lesser, or mild, ginger) is native to China, although the Chinese use neither in their cooking (they are sometimes used in medicinal infusions). Both types are used in Indonesia, Malaysia, and Thailand. The two types can be used interchangeably. Fresh or frozen galangal is best.

Ginger

A rhizome, ginger is available either young or mature. In its young form, it is spicy, tender, juicy, and bright yellow, with a translucent pinkish yellow skin. The more-available mature ginger has a dull and tan-colored skin. Its meat is also less bright and more fibrous than that of the young rhizome. If a recipe calls for ginger juice, simply grate a piece of ginger and squeeze the pulp over a sieve set on a bowl, extracting the juice in the process. Collect the juice and discard the pulp left in the sieve. *Note: Young ginger, because it is less fibrous and has more water content than the mature type, will yield more juice (possibly double) per ounce (about 2 tablespoons) than mature ginger. Every ounce of ginger should give you at least 1 to 2 tablespoons juice. Young ginger rhizomes are available in Asian markets, natural foods stores, and occasionally in Western farmers' markets. If you find them, buy a pound and make pickled ginger (see page 54).*

Grapeseed Oil

Extracted from the seeds of grapes in Europe and the United States, grapeseed oil is now widely available. It has the same health benefits as olive oil, but it can take higher cooking temperatures. It is an ideal all-purpose cooking oil that can be used in salad dressings, marinades, and stir-fries, or for deep-frying. I prefer grapeseed oil to peanut oil, which is generally used in Asian cookery, because it is light and mild in flavor. In my recipes I generically call for "vegetable oil." Grapeseed oil is it for me.

Hoisin Sauce

Mostly sweet, with a salty back note, hoisin sauce is a thick soybean paste that is dark brown in color. With mild hints of garlic, sesame, vinegar, and chili, this sauce is used for marinating all sorts of meats, giving them a reddish hue when cooked. (Koon Chun)

Hot Bean Paste

A spicy, ruby red, and very smooth hot soybean paste also called *kochujang*. A Korean hot chili condiment, it has a thick misolike texture, and is used as a dipping sauce when mixed with honey and rice vinegar, and as flavoring agent for soups, stir-fries, grilled foods, and braised dishes. (Choripdong or Wang)

Kaffir Lime Leaves

The leaves that make Thai food unmistakably Thai, these can be found fresh at Southeast Asian markets or upscale markets. Kaffir lime leaves lend an earthy, lemony, floral note to curries and soups. I also enjoy them in marinades or herbal tea infusions, or for making an herbal broth. They can be bought fresh or frozen, and these are best. They can also be purchased dried.

Kelp

The word *kelp* is also used to described various types of brown algae, but it usually refers to Japanese *kombu,* or giant kelp. It grows about a foot a day and can reach several hundred feet in length. It is the basis for the Japanese stock known as dashi. It is also cut in pieces and fried, or soaked in water until pliable and added to seaweed salads or soups. It is almost always purchased dried. Be sure to wipe it with a damp cloth prior to using.

Lemongrass

A very fibrous herb with a floral citrus flavor, lemongrass grows in clumps and is used in Cambodian, Indonesian, Vietnamese, and Thai cuisines. The entire stalk can be used in cooking, the creamy white bulb section (with purple rings) being the most pungent. The light green top part can be used in soup stocks or herbal infusions. Prior to using, be sure to peel off the outer leaves and trim the root end, as well as 2 to 3 inches of the dark green top. Lemongrass freezes well. Do not wash prior to refrigerating or freezing. To freeze, simply wrap individual stalks in aluminum foil. *Note: Dried lemongrass is a poor substitute because it is just about flavorless.*

Lotus Leaves

Large and round, lotus leaves are used in Asian cooking for wrapping foods, including sticky rice dishes. They impart a wonderfully bitter tealike flavor. Lotus leaves are available dried and must be soaked until rehydrated before using. They can be purchased at Asian markets and by mail order.

Mirin

This is basically sweetened sake, or rice wine, without the alcohol content. Sold in Asian, natural foods, and gourmet markets, mirin is used in marinades, braised foods, dipping sauces, and salad dressings. If you cannot find mirin, make a simple syrup using two parts sake to one part sugar, and simmer until the alcohol has evaporated completely and the liquids have thickened slightly. (Mikawa Organic Mirin)

Miso

There are about two hundred types of miso used in Japan. A soybean paste similar to Chinese hoisin sauce, yet very different in flavor—it's salty as opposed to sweet, with a deep fermented flavor—miso is used in soups, stews, salad dressings, and marinades. The three basic types are white (tan in color), red (brown in color), and black (dark brown in color). White miso, known as shiro-miso, is the mildest of them all, having a slightly sweet taste. It is a perfect starting point for the cook who is not familiar with the product. The darker the miso, the saltier and more robust in flavor it is. Red miso is known as aka-miso, and black miso is known as hatcho-miso. (Miso Master Organic or Cold Mountain or Hanamaruki)

Mung Beans, Yellow

These are green mung beans that have been peeled and split. I highly recommend you purchase these as opposed to whole green mung beans. Removing the skins is tedious work.

Nori

A type of seaweed (or sea vegetable), nori is available in various forms at Asian and natural foods stores. Use nori flakes for garnishing rice, and nori sheets for making sushi. Many brands are imported from Japan, but the United States now produces organic types that are more readily available in markets throughout the country. (Eden)

Palm Sugar

Harvested from the abundant Asian coconut palm tree, palm sugar is used in savory and sweet Asian foods. Sold in plastic tubs imported from Thailand, this semisoft tan paste lends a subtle coconut flavor to foods.

Peanuts

Originating in South America, peanuts are also referred to as groundnuts. For Asian cooking, you will need unsalted roasted peanuts to make peanut sauce or to use crushed as a garnish. If you are allergic to peanuts, try unsalted roasted cashews as a substitute. Nuts turn rancid quickly because of their high oil content. Store in an airtight jar in a dark, cool place for 3 to 4 months, or refrigerate for up to 6 months.

Pickled Ginger

Made from young ginger rhizomes, pickled ginger is readily available sliced, shredded, or minced. (The pinker the color, the more coloring has been added.) While it can be bought in gourmet shops, natural foods stores, and Asian markets, or via mail order, it is quite easy to make pickled ginger at home. I highly recommend this approach when young ginger is available. It takes no time at all, and requires only four ingredients: young ginger, salt, sugar, and rice vinegar (see page 54).

Potato Starch Noodles

Also known as cellophane or glass noodles, potato starch noodles are a specialty of Korea and Japan. (Chinese types are thinner and made with mung bean starch.) Korean potato starch noodles are round, slightly uneven, long, and translucent gray, while the Japanese types are white, straight, and squareish. All turn transparent when cooked. Soak until pliable prior to cooking. Available at Asian markets or by mail order.

Preserved Lemons

While you can buy these in brine at Middle Eastern or Asian markets, they are easy to make at home (see page 55), and are far less expensive and much more fragrant than the store-bought types.

Rice

Many rice varieties exist and are categorized as short, medium, long, white, brown, red, black, sticky (or "glutinous"). Long-grain jasmine rice is the everyday rice in China and Southeast Asia. In Japan and Korea, the short- to medium-grain "sushi" variety is the most common. Sticky short-grain rice is used occasionally, wrapped in leaves and cooked in broth or water. See chapter 4, "Flat Breads, Rice, and Noodles," for instructions on how to cook different types of rice, from long-grain jasmine or basmati, to short- or medium-grain "sushi" rice, to the sticky short-grain type.

Rice Vermicelli

Perfect for light summer fare, these white noodles are the thickness of cappellini (angel hair pasta). They are used for tossing with vegetables and dressing, in soups, or stir-fries. Readily available, there are several brands to choose from. (Erawan "Three Elephant" or Thai Market)

Rice Vinegar

Rice vinegar is mild compared to white wine vinegar. It is the basic vinegar for all Asian cooking. You can use Chinese or Japanese rice wine vinegar interchangeably. Be sure to use plain, not seasoned, rice vinegar. Rice vinegar is a great substitute for coconut vinegar, if you cannot find the latter. (Swatow, Narcissus, Marukan, or Mitsukan)

Sake

A Japanese rice wine, similar to Chinese Shaoxing rice wine, but generally more refined. Sake is drunk chilled, at room temperature, or heated. It also gives food a wonderful flavor. Use sake in sauces for braising or dipping, or marinades. There are hundreds to choose from. Like all wines used in cooking, the sake you choose should be good enough to drink.

Scallions

Also known as green onions, scallions are immature onions. Like garlic and ginger, they play a great role in Asian cuisines. After trimming the root end and the last inch or so of the green tops, the entire stalk (white to dark green) is edible.

Scallions can be bruised or lightly crushed and added to stocks, or sliced and added to any number of dishes cooked or raw.

Sesame Oil, Dark

Asian sesame oil, made from toasted sesame seeds, is dark amber in color and very pungent. Use in small quantities so as not to overwhelm the palate and mask the other flavor notes in your food. (Kadoya)

Sesame Seeds

While there are several varieties of sesame seeds, the most commonly used in Asian cooking are white (raw or toasted) and black. They are most often used as a last-minute garnish, imparting a nutty flavor and crunchy texture. Sesame seeds have a high oil content and turn rancid fast. Store in an air-tight jar for 3 to 4 months in a dark, cool place, or up to 6 months in the refrigerator. *Note: To toast sesame seeds (or nuts like walnuts), put the seeds in a dry skillet over low heat and shake the pan until the seeds are golden, not burnt.*

Shallots

Small and purplish gray or brown in color, shallots are widely used in Asian cooking as a last-minute garnish, either fried or raw, or in stir-fries or braised foods. In a pinch, you can use red onion. I like using shallots rather than onions when they are available because I generally find them to be sweeter than onions. On a practical level, if I only need a small amount of onion for a recipe, shallots are the perfect size.

Shaoxing (Chinese) Rice Wine

There are many Chinese rice wines to choose from. Make sure to use the unseasoned kind, not those labeled "cooking wine." Sake is a perfect substitute for Shaoxing rice wine.

Shiitake Mushrooms, Dried

These come in all sizes and in a variety of colors, from light whitish tan to dark brownish black, and from thick to thin. Generally speaking, use the inexpensive thin, dark mushrooms for sauces or soups. For braised dishes where the mushrooms are served whole, buy the more expensive thick, meaty whitish tan types. Very fragrant (more so than the fresh ones; see below), dried shiitakes must be soaked in water until rehydrated and very soft. The amount of time for soaking depends largely on the temperature of the water (warmer water accelerates the softening process) and the thickness of the mushroom. For thin types, figure 30 minutes in lukewarm water, for the thick ones 1 hour or more. Soaking them overnight, 12 or more hours, will not hurt them. Store in an airtight container in a cool, dark place.

Shiitake Mushrooms, Fresh

These very popular mushrooms are available year-round at most markets. The woody stems are generally removed and discarded prior to cooking. The flavor of fresh shiitakes tends to be milder than that of their dried counterpart (see above), where the flavor is concentrated through the curing process.

Shiso Leaves

Packaged about ten leaves per pack, shiso leaves (purple or green) are heart shaped, with serrated edges. They are found in Japanese and Korean markets, and through mail-order sources. The plants are self-sowing annuals, but they are invasive and can take over your garden, just like mint.

Shrimp Paste

Available in Southeast Asian markets and by mail order, shrimp paste is sold in round plastic containers and imported from Thailand *(kepi),* or in rectangular blocks wrapped in paper and imported from Indonesia *(terasi)* or Malaysia *(balacan).* The strong aroma will take over your refrigerator unless you wrap, wrap, and wrap this food again. I wrap my shrimp block in plastic before putting it in a wide-mouthed glass jar, which I then store in the freezer. (Klong Kone "prawn in red sun" or Balachen)

Soba Noodles

Made from buckwheat flour, soba is a specialty of northern Japan. Available dried or fresh-frozen, soba comes in a variety of flavors, including buckwheat, pink plum, and green tea. All are delicious and can be used alone or combined for colorful food presentations.

Soy Sauce, Mushroom

A soy sauce with pungent straw mushroom extract added to it, this is a wonderful seasoning, especially with heavier red meats such as beef, buffalo, lamb, ostrich, or duck. (Healthy, a.k.a. "Baby" Boy)

Soy Sauce, Thick

Used primarily as a colorant in Chinese cooking, this soy sauce is generally employed in small quantities. Sweetened with molasses, it is always combined with thin soy sauce (see below) in marinades. (Koon Chun)

Soy Sauce, Thin

Thin soy sauce is used as a seasoning all over Asia (specifically in China, Japan, and Korea). In Southeast Asian countries—where fish sauce is the equivalent seasoning of choice—soy sauce is used by strict vegetarians and Buddhist monks. (Wan Ja Shan, Koon Chun, or Marudaizu Organic)

Sunchokes (Jerusalem Artichokes)

A native American tuber, the sunchoke is related to the sunflower, and has nothing to do with Jerusalem or artichokes. I must confess, however, that the tuber does taste a bit like artichoke hearts. Sunchokes look like a cross between a tuber and a rhizome (like ginger, for example), and are a bit gnarly in appearance. Although available year-round, they are best during the late fall, winter, and early spring. They are delicious raw or cooked. Refrigerate for up to 2 weeks.

Tamari

This used to be the only soy sauce made without using wheat as a fermenting agent. It was developed in Japan for eating with sushi and sashimi. *If you are allergic to wheat, please check the label carefully, as some tamari sauces now include wheat as a fermenting agent.*

Tamarind

This fruit is available fresh in its brittle, beanlike brown pod, packaged as pulp (generally 16 ounces), or as a concentrate. I like to use the fresh fruit straight from the pod or the packaged pulp for making my own concentrate (page 55). In a pinch, however, use the concentrate as a reliable (but not quite as delicious) time-saver.

Tangerine Peel

Dried tangerine peel can be found in Asian markets or can be mail-ordered. If you want to make your own, use the same technique as for making dried lemons (see page 21). This time, however, use only the zest, or colored part, of the peel, removed with a vegetable peeler or paring knife.

Tapioca Pearls

Found in Asian markets, tapioca pearls come in small, medium, and large sizes, and in white, pink, or green colors. They are made from the cassava root.

Thai Basil

Licorice-like in flavor, these dark green pointy leaves (attached to purplish green stems) are used extensively in Southeast Asian foods. There is no substitute. If you are unable to find this herb, omit it entirely. Thai basil is available at Asian markets or through mail-order sources.

Thai Chilies

Red or green, these are about an 8 to 9 on a heat scale of 1 to 10. They are about 1½ inches long and slightly less than ¼ inch in diameter at the widest (stem) end. Widely known as Thai chilies, they are also referred to as finger, bird's eye, or bird chilies, although the latter correctly refers to a much smaller type of chili that has a bit more heat. I like to use the red Thai chilies because herbs are generally green and the red lends a nice contrasting color. Nowadays, you can also find hybrid Thai chilies measuring 3 to 4 inches long and about ½ inch wide. The heat from the larger chilies is less intense, but they are more readily available than the small ones, unless you do your shopping in Chinatown. You can also use habanero or Scotch bonnet chilies, although these are much spicier, not to mention different in flavor. About one-third of a habanero or Scotch bonnet will do for every Thai chili. Sometimes, fresh cayenne peppers can be found; these resemble the larger of the two Thai chilies in size and heat scale. In general, remove the seeds from chili pods to reduce the heat level.

Tofu

Tofu comes in several types: silken, soft, medium-firm, firm, and extra-firm (also known as "pressed"). Some are grainy in texture and come in plastic tubs; others are "silken" and come in a carton similar to milk cartons. When grilling, I like to use firm tofu, which has just enough moisture to keep the pieces from drying out. Firm tofu also retains its shape well when flipped.

Turmeric

Also known as Indian saffron, native to Southeast Asia and used as a dye for millennia, turmeric is a small, thin rhizome with a brownish skin and yellowish orange meat. Turmeric is so mild in flavor that it is prized almost singularly as a colorant, giving foods a deep yellow color, as in curry powder. Turmeric is available fresh and frozen, but is mostly used dried as a powder. If you happen to find the fresh or frozen rhizomes, note that they are best when pounded into herbal pastes; they offer a bit more fragrance than their dried counterpart.

Wasabi

Wasabi is a Japanese mustard root most often appearing as a green paste accompanying sushi and sashimi in Japanese restaurants. Fresh wasabi root is green, and can now be increasingly found in Japanese markets in the United States. Although fresh is the best, especially when grated, it is very expensive (about $25 for a 3- to 4-inch piece). The next best thing is the dried powder form, which makes a nice paste by mixing 2 parts wasabi powder to 1 part water. I do not recommend the wasabi sold in tubes; its texture and flavor are inferior, and it is generally adulterated with green food coloring as well as other additives.

Yogurt, Greek

Excellent for eating straight from the container or for creating delicious recipes, Greek yogurt has no substitute. It is thick and rich, with none of the additives commonly used in other yogurts (whether organic or not). Greek yogurt is especially wonderful for making dips to which vinegar or lemon juice is added, because the yogurt retains its thickness even when stirred. (Other yogurts, generally containing gums and other additives, turn to liquid after stirring just a few times, making these poor substitutes.) The brand I like best comes with various concentrations of fat: 0%, 2%, 4%, and full fat. All of them are excellent, and even the nonfat is very rich and creamy in texture and flavor. (Total).

CHAPTER 2

GRILLING TOOLS, GRILLS, AND COOKING TIPS

I am often asked how much money one needs to spend on grilling equipment in order to cook properly. My answer is "whatever makes you comfortable," cautioning that "more" and "fancy" are not always better. "Buy what is actually useful to you, and don't overcrowd your space with unnecessary gadgets" is also part of my advice. In many parts of Asia, one all-purpose knife, a cutting board, and chopsticks are considered sufficient tools. A cooking surface may consist of four bricks with a metal grill grate.

GRILLING TOOLS

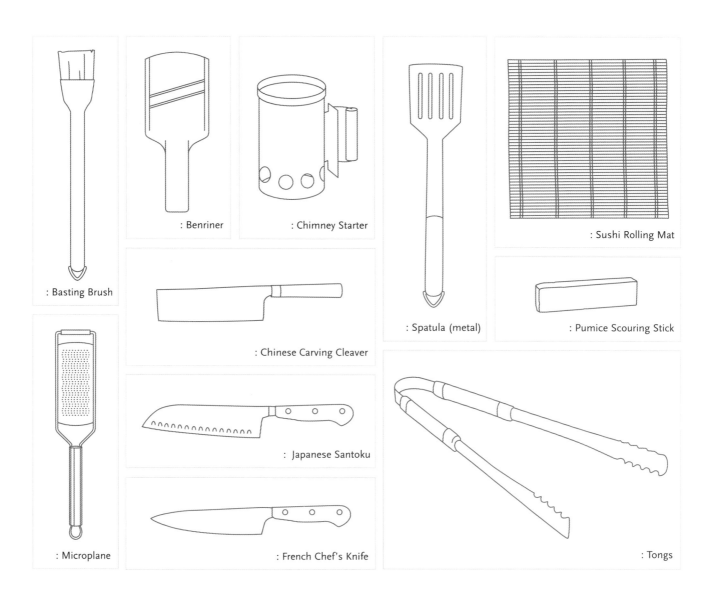

: Benriner

: Chimney Starter

: Sushi Rolling Mat

: Basting Brush

: Chinese Carving Cleaver

: Spatula (metal)

: Pumice Scouring Stick

: Japanese Santoku

: Microplane

: French Chef's Knife

: Tongs

Kindling (minus any toxic chemical starter) and small pieces of firewood may be all that is used for a heat source in the form of coals. Much of what qualifies as a "kitchen" is often very, very basic, and the food is usually fantastic. I have never had a bad meal prepared at a home, in a restaurant, or on a sidewalk anywhere in Asia. Minimum fuss, a structured approach to cooking, and fresh ingredients are the key.

GRILLING TOOLS AND MORE

Here are my recommendations for a few simple tools that will go a long way to ensure successful grilling and cooking in general.

Basting Brush

A basting brush is great to have, but a spoon can work in a pinch.

Benriner

A Japanese mandoline. Made of sturdy, hard plastic, it comes with three blades for slicing different thicknesses, and a removable box for collecting the julienned vegetables. It is easy to use, comfortable in the hand, and fairly inexpensive. It is a fraction of the cost of the French stainless-steel mandoline—a cumbersome tool that can be difficult to use.

Chimney Starter

This is a great tool for starting charcoal fires. Essentially a cylinder-shaped container with air holes and a handle, it holds charcoal on the topside and has a space for paper or kindling on the underside. Simply use a match to light the crumpled paper and watch the charcoal quickly become engulfed in flames. Wait about 15 minutes, and when the charcoal is red and covered with white ash, dump the burning charcoal into the fuel bed of the grill.

Chinese Carving Cleaver, Japanese Santoku, and French Chef's Knife

The Chinese carving cleaver has a blade that is about 2 inches wide and 7 to 8 inches long, with a square tip. The Japanese santoku (from the Japanese word meaning "three good things": slicing, dicing, and mincing) is derived from the Chinese carving cleaver, and has a broad (1¾ inches wide), thick single- or thin double-sided bevel-edged blade that is about 7 inches in length and has a squarish rounded tip. The double-sided bevel edge comes flat or with hollows, and with or without a Damascus finish, to keep food from clinging. This knife is increasingly popular in the West. In addition to Japanese-made versions, it is now being manufactured by companies such as Wüsthof and Henckels. The French chef's knife has a pointed tip, with blades of varying lengths: 7, 8, 9, and 10 inches.

Note: There are very significant price differences between and among these knives, ranging from under ten dollars to several hundred dollars. I own several types purchased at several different prices. All work wonderfully, and more expensive is not always better. One of my favorite blades is the Chinese carving cleaver (traditionally used for slicing Peking duck). I picked one up in New York City's Chinatown for about five dollars several years ago, and I'm still using it. Select a blade size and weight that fit your hand and keep the knife sharp.

Grill Brush

A metal grill brush is used to scrub the grill grate clean before and after grilling. In a pinch, crumple a piece of aluminum foil (heavy-duty foil works best) and, holding it with tongs, scrub the grill grate.

Microplane

The best tool for finely grating is the popular Microplane, which can be found at any kitchen supply place. Some have interchangeable blades for various consistencies. For fibrous ingredients like lemongrass and mature ginger, use a fine Microplane. Microplaning also releases the ingredient's essence more easily than a regular grater.

Pumice Scouring Stick

Use this when the grill grate has been neglected and the buildup is just too much for a grill brush (or crumpled aluminum foil) to handle. Pumice sticks are very inexpensive, come in different grades, and can be found in hardware stores. Make sure that yours is wet enough to form a paste to minimize scratching.

Spatula, Metal

Good for flipping large fish fillets on the grill.

Sushi Rolling Mat

While you can roll maki (sushi rolls) by hand, a sushi rolling mat makes the task much easier and ensures a beautiful, even roll. A great kitchen tool made of super-thin bamboo sticks woven together with cotton string, the mat is readily available and very inexpensive. You can make all sorts of maki, both savory and sweet, with this handy tool.

Tongs

An enormously useful tool. Buy tongs in two lengths (short and long) and make sure that they are fairly light in weight (these can also be used for foods cooked on a stove). Good tongs should be easy to handle and should feel comfortable in the hand. Many commercial "grilling" tongs tend to be oversized, heavy, and ultimately too awkward (and sometimes a bit painful) to hold for any length of time. Spring-loaded tongs are my all-purpose tool, wonderful for flipping, turning, shuffling, and grabbing food.

GRILLS

Charcoal Grills

The key to a great charcoal grill is simplicity. I like the no-fuss charcoal grills that Weber manufactures. They are generally round and come in several sizes and colors. I own two, a 14½-inch-diameter one for the city, where I grill on my fire escape, and a huge 37½-inch-diameter one for the country, where I entertain quite a bit and like to smoke foods occasionally. Other sizes are available at all sorts of stores, including hardware stores, and via mail order. It usually takes very little time—15 to 25 minutes—to get a charcoal fire started and build a bed of coals for grilling. The hottest part of the grill is directly above the heat source. The more removed from the heat source the food is, the lower the temperature (see "Indirect-Heat Grilling" page 34). You can easily judge the temperature by how fast the food is cooking. If it is burning, the heat is too high. Move the food toward a cooler area of the grill so as not to burn it. Grill fire temperatures are controlled by spreading the coals out, by raising or lowering the grill top, or by opening or closing the vents. Judge the temperature by holding your hand, palm side down, over the grill grate above the heat source. If you can only hold it for 1 to 2 seconds, it is hot; at 3 to 4 seconds, the fire is medium-hot, while 5 seconds or more is low. Note that a grill thermometer is available as an option on some grills, but many cooks develop an intuitive or habitual feel for grill cooking.

Gas Grills

Many people like a gas grill for its convenience. Using one is arguably less messy than handling charcoal, but you have to clean the grill grate, just as with a charcoal grill, and you have to remember to get the propane tank filled and to turn it off when you are done. Contrary to popular belief, you also have to heat the grill top, just as with a charcoal grill. Turning the flame on and immediately placing the meat on the grill is not the way to start. You must turn on the flame, cover the grill, and wait the same 15 to 25 minutes it would take to build a fire for a charcoal grill in order to heat the grill, burn off any buildup, and allow you to scrub the grill with a grill brush. In other words, in many circumstances a gas grill takes just as much time to prep as a well-maintained and -stocked charcoal grill. If you prefer a gas grill, however, look for a durable one that has a proper exit pathway for flammable fat and grease to avoid flare-ups, and that offers an even distribution of heat so that all the food on the grill cooks evenly. The Weber Summit (I used it for gas-grill recipe testing for this book) is a very good choice.

The Fire Pit

Every once in a while, digging a fire pit for a grill party is fun. I've done it at the beach with friends and everyone got involved, making it part of the festivities. Pick a location that is far away from any vegetation or other flammables, and, if you are in a public area, make sure that you have the right to have an open fire and that you have secured any required permits. Bring a grill grate (Weber's 22½-inch one for example) and build a bowl-shaped pit so that the grate will fit comfortably at the top of the stone-lined pit with about 8 inches of clearance below for a bed of coals (2 to 3 inches) and an air buffer. Fire pits will vary in size of course, but a 22½-inch grate would work well with a 12-inch-deep pit about 24 inches in diameter. Line the pit with a single layer of roundish flat stones (1 to 2 inches thick) so that they just touch. Set the stones all the way up the sides of the pit to the top, reducing the diameter enough for your grill grate to fit. (If it doesn't fit, adjust the pit a bit.) Arrange some twigs or other kindling in teepee fashion in the center of the pit, starting with smaller pieces and building to larger pieces of firewood. (Place a few sheets of crumpled paper at the center at this point, if you wish.) Set the firewood loosely (air space will allow you to light the innermost ring and get you air for feeding the fire) and always keep the teepee form. It is a good idea to place almost all of your wood on the fire before you light it, because the inner flame will heat and dry the outside layers of firewood as it burns (see notes on wood, right). Light

your fire with a long match—you want to get in toward the center—protecting it from the wind as required. Depending on the species and moisture content of your firewood, it will take about 45 minutes to 1 hour for the wood to burn down to red-hot coals. Once the fire burns down, spread the hot coals evenly across the bottom of the pit with a shovel, and place the grill grate on top of the stone edge, allowing it to heat. Place your food on the grill and follow the recipe instructions from there. You can either keep the food items uncovered, or form a lid with banana leaves (see Asian Clambake, page 104) for a smoky note. If everything has been properly prepared, the coals should stay hot for several hours. *Note: Always keep a fire extinguisher or a source of water handy, and have an emergency plan in case of accidents.*

Cooking with Wood

I love building wood-fueled cooking fires. From gathering the kindling and firewood, to lighting the fire and placing the grill grate, it allows you to richly experience the day and enjoy the night sky, and seems to go well with sipping a great Cognac as the last embers die away long after dinner. You can build a wood fire in a fire pit or a charcoal grill. Always use hardwoods, such as oak, ash, and maple. Birch, and especially its bark, makes for great kindling, burning with a sweet smell. Cherry, apple, and other fruit woods can lend a fruity note, especially when smoking foods (see page 34). Don't use soft woods (evergreens, such as pine) as they burn very quickly and are full of tar. Build your wood fire in the shape of a teepee in the fuel bed of a charcoal grill. When the wood has burnt down, spread the red-hot coals in an even layer, and place the grill grate above.

For kindling, use small dry twigs from hardwood trees, grapevines or other vines, or birch bark. Arrange them in a teepee formation (to allow air to pass up through and out-ward) and light them with a match. Burning newspaper and cardboard releases toxic dioxins into the atmosphere. Birch bark is my preferred starter when it is available. Solid-fuel nontoxic starters are preferable to liquid chemical starters.

If your fire needs a boost, never squirt lighter fluid on it; use wood lightly splashed with vegetable or other cooking oil. While many people like to gradually add small or split logs to the fire as it burns, the best way to build a fire is to place as much of the wood fuel on it as possible when you are first stacking it up. A clean, hot fire is best, and this practice concentrates the heat, drying the unburned fuel as it goes, protecting it from wind, fully combusting the wood and its gases, and minimizing air pollution, while allowing the progressively larger pieces of wood to fall into the center.

If you need to replenish the wood, place it on the outside and let it combust and fall into the center. When you have a good amount of coals, knock the fire down into an even, flat bed. (You can also create a wood fire in an outdoor fireplace or fire pit and later transfer the coals to a charcoal grill with a metal coal, or similarly broad, shovel. Use extreme caution when doing this—it is easy to get burned or unintentionally spread the fire.) For judging the temperature of your fire, see "Charcoal Grills" page 32.

DIRECT- AND INDIRECT-HEAT GRILLING

Direct-Heat Grilling
Direct-heat grilling simply means grilling directly over the heat source, whether you are using a gas or charcoal grill. If using a charcoal grill, be sure that the coals form an even layer to ensure equal heat throughout.

Indirect-Heat Grilling
Indirect-heat grilling means grilling on a hot grill, but not directly over the heat source. Generally, you push the coals over to one side and grill on the opposite side, with the grill cover on. In the case of very large foods, you should push the coals to opposite sides of the grill. This type of fire will slow-cook the ingredients and give them a nice smoky flavor. To cook by indirect heat on a gas grill, turn on the gas on one side of the grill, and place the food on the opposite side.

COOKING TIPS

Marinating
Food is marinated to impart flavor before cooking. Marinating is done either at room temperature or in the refrigerator. Note that cool temperatures slow down the speed at which a marinade penetrates a protein. Over-marinating makes a food overly salty and kills its flavor. Undermarinating will fail to flavor the food.

The smaller the cut of food, the faster the marinade will penetrate it. Slices or bite-size cubes of meat should generally marinate for about 30 minutes at room temperature or 1 hour in the refrigerator. Large cuts, fatty cuts, and solid cuts of meat require longer marinating times. A 12-ounce steak, for example, can marinate for 1 hour at room temperature or 2 hours refrigerated. Chicken thighs with the skin on will require a slightly longer marinating time than skinless chicken breasts. A very large cut of meat, such as a whole leg of lamb, can marinate for 24 hours in the refrigerator. For fish such as tuna or swordfish, and crustaceans and mollusks such as shrimp, lobster, and squid, use the same marinating principles as for poultry. For delicate seafood such as flounder, sea bass fillets, or scallops, marinate for about 30 minutes. No flesh food should be marinated at room temperature for more than 2 hours. If you want to marinate it longer, refrigerate the food. That said, all seafood should marinate in the refrigerator.

Freezing
Freezing is a great way to prep a meal ahead of time for those who have a busy lifestyle. If you are not going to freeze a properly marinated food, you have to cook it right away to prevent spoilage. Freezing a marinated raw food will stop the marinating process. You can continue marinating the food after it has defrosted. After thawing completely, cook the meat as you would any food marinated at room temperature or refrigerated. Overnight refrigerator thawing is recommended.

Cooking Temperatures

All proteins should be at room temperature prior to grilling. Otherwise, they will not cook evenly. A rare steak, for example, will look cooked on the outside but be cold and raw on the inside if it wasn't first brought to room temperature. Depending on the cut of meat (sliced, cubed, or large cuts), you will need 30 minutes to 1 hour to bring it to room temperature after refrigeration.

Doneness Temperatures

Ground Meat and Meat Mixtures

    Beef, pork, veal, lamb: 160°F
    Turkey, chicken: 165°F

Fresh Beef, Veal, Lamb

    Medium-rare: 145°F
    Medium: 160°F
    Well-done: 170°F

Chicken

    Breasts: 170°F
    Thighs, wings: 180°F

Duck Breast/Legs

    Medium-rare: 145°F
    Medium: 160°F
    Well-done: 170°F
    Legs: 180°F

Fresh Pork

    Medium: 160°F
    Well-done: 170°F

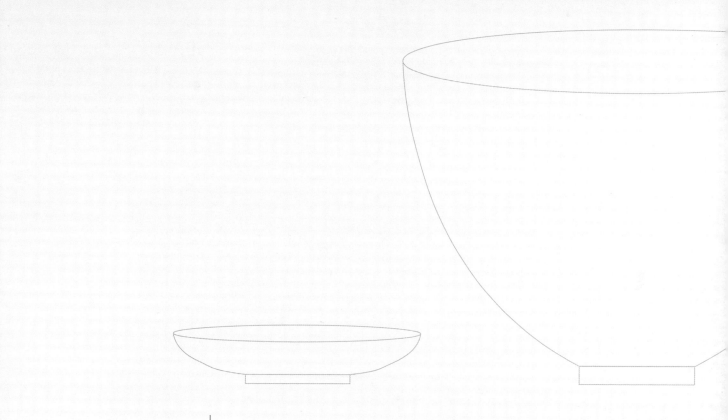

CHAPTER 3 | CONDIMENTS

The English word *condiment* dates from the fifteenth century, but any decent ancient Roman house cook would have recognized the Latin word *condimentum* as meaning "to season." Condiments are any foodstuffs used to season and enhance food flavors, but especially those that are pungent. Condiments are essential to grilling—the art of the grill is largely the art of condiments.

In this book, marinades, spice pastes, and dry rubs and salad dressings are considered condiments. Bottled (or jarred) Asian sauces, such as soy sauce, fish sauce, or chili paste, are also indispensable. So are relishes and a variety of dipping sauces. Pastes—essentially mashed and blended herbs—can be used as is or be added to marinades, sometimes with dry spices in the mix as well. You will also find savory yogurts. Please note that while pickles are condiments, I have chosen to place them in the vegetable chapter.

Condiments are either applied before cooking (pastes, rubs, or marinades), or are used as flavor enhancers after cooking (dipping sauces and other sauces and dressings), for what I call the "finishing note," meant to give a little kick at the end of the bite. When applied before cooking, condiments can be powerful, essentially extending the range of your cooking by transforming the ingredient completely. Condiments applied after cooking tend to color the ingredient, adding flavor notes and refreshing the palate.

Some condiments are best when fresh, especially during the warmest months of the year when they are meant to refresh the palate. For this reason, when time allows, I try to prepare them the morning of the day I will be grilling. My yellow spice paste is made with galangal and lemongrass, for example, and it is always best when made just a few hours ahead of time, allowing the flavors to blend while still making it possible to taste each ingredient separately. Let's face it, some things improve with age, some things do not. Fresh versions of some condiments will make all the difference, while with others not so much so. I note the time-critical ones in my recipes and assure you that the results will be well worth the effort.

Many condiment recipes are absolutely fine when made a week ahead of time. If a recipe contains sugar, salt, and vinegar—three of the best preserving and curing agents—then the chances are it will keep for a week in the refrigerator without too much flavor loss. Just remember that the longer a sauce sits, the more the ingredients are cured. The clean flavor you had on day one will be diminished a bit on day two, more on day three, and so on. This is not to say that the results will be bad, just that they will be different.

To get maximum flavor from your concoctions, remember that many bottled condiments are fine—some can be fantastic. You can build a wonderful, and more importantly, essential Asian pantry with readily available bottled and jarred condiments, such as thin soy sauce, thick soy sauce, fish sauce, sesame oil, rice vinegar, miso, and chili-garlic sauce. These will be the basis for your many homemade concoctions. Some condiments can be made at home, frozen, and thawed when needed.

Asians often think of salads as a part of a dish rather than as a separate dish. This is not to say that Asian flavors cannot work on Western-style salads. Quite the contrary, I have created two Asian salad dressings with miso, ginger, and rice vinegar as the base. Either is wonderful tossed with leafy greens or beans, or even potatoes. You can also use these miso-based salad dressings as dipping sauces for any grilled food.

MISO SALAD DRESSING OR DIPPING SAUCE

Makes about 1 cup

One of my favorite ways to serve baby salad greens is to toss them with this Japanese–inspired miso–based dressing. Light and refreshing, it celebrates the complex flavors of some of Asia's most popular condiments without being over-whelming. Sweet and salty with shiro–miso, tangy with rice vinegar, smoky with dark sesame oil, and mildly spicy with freshly grated ginger, the recipe is perfect for the baby greens. Try it as a dipping sauce for grilled meats and Grilled Vegetables (page 93), too.

¼ cup shiro-miso (white miso)

¼ cup mirin (sweet sake)

¼ cup rice vinegar

2 teaspoons dark sesame oil

2 tablespoons vegetable oil

1 to 1½ tablespoons finely grated fresh ginger or ginger juice (see page 22)

1 scallion, trimmed and minced (white and green parts)

In a salad bowl, whisk together the shiro-miso, mirin, and rice vinegar until smooth. Add the sesame and vegetable oils, ginger, and scallion and stir until well combined. This sauce is best freshly made. Refrigerate for up to 3 days.

NOTE: As a rule of thumb, I generally toss 4 to 5 cups of salad greens to about ¼ cup of dressing; that's about 1 tablespoon of dressing to 1 cup of leafy greens. The result is a subtle hint of the dressing, allowing you to enjoy the natural fla-vor of the leafy greens, or any other type of vegetable you choose.

LEMON-AND-GINGER-INFUSED SOY SAUCE

Makes about 2 cups

Essentially a classic Japanese ponzu sauce, this pungent, sweet, and salty sauce is a delicious complement to maki (sushi rolls) such as the Grilled Wild Salmon Sushi Rolls (page 109). Versatile, it can also be used as a dipping sauce, marinade, or basting liquid for all sorts of grilled seafood, poultry, and meats. It can be made days, even weeks, ahead of time.

1¼ cups thin soy sauce

1   cup sake

¾   cup mirin (sweet sake)

    Juice of 4 lemons (about ¾ cup)

½   cup rice vinegar

¼   cup tamari

½   cup plus 2 tablespoons sugar

6   large garlic cloves, crushed

5   scallions, trimmed, halved, and crushed (white and green parts)

¼   cup thinly sliced fresh ginger

    One 2-by-4-inch piece kombu (kelp), wiped with damp cloth

1. In a large bowl, whisk together the soy sauce, sake, mirin, lemon juice, rice vinegar, tamari, and sugar until the sugar is completely dissolved.

2. Add the garlic, scallions, ginger, and kombu and mix well.

3. Transfer to a saucepan and simmer over low heat until reduced to 3⅔ cups, about 2 hours. Remove the sauce from the heat and let it cool completely. Pour the sauce through a sieve set over a jar. Discard the solids, close the jar, and refrigerate for up to 6 months.

SPICY PEANUT SAUCE

Makes about 5 cups

2 tablespoons vegetable oil

1½ to 2 tablespoons red curry paste

1 tablespoon shrimp paste

1½ cups unsalted roasted peanuts, finely ground

¼ cup palm sugar or granulated sugar

2 cups unsweetened coconut milk

2 cups chicken broth (recipe follows)

½ cup Tamarind Concentrate (page 55)

3 tablespoons hoisin sauce

½ cup packed fresh Thai basil leaves, minced

½ cup packed fresh cilantro leaves, minced

This recipe combines fresh herbs and other ingredients used in classic Vietnamese, Thai, and Indonesian peanut sauces to create a new one that celebrates all the classic versions. As a result, it is rich and full of complexity, yet does not overwhelm the palate. It starts out sweet, with the caramelized palm sugar, goes on to earthy coconut and peanut flavors, refreshes the palate with licorice-like Thai basil and lemony cilantro, with some heat on the finish from the Thai curry paste, which packs quite a bit of its own herbal flavor blend, including lemongrass and galangal. This peanut sauce is also relatively light, using half the coconut milk of most peanut sauces and replacing it with chicken broth, as is traditionally done in parts of Vietnam. This sauce is delicious with grilled meats such as classic satay, but can be used with wraps as well. My friends like to eat it by the spoonful, too.

In a saucepan, heat the oil over medium heat. Add the curry paste and stir-fry until fragrant, about 2 minutes. Add the shrimp paste and continue to stir-fry until the shrimp paste is broken up and one shade darker, about 1 minute. Add the peanuts and stir, roasting until two shades darker but not burnt, 8 to 10 minutes. Add the sugar and continue to stir-fry until the sugar is dissolved and starts to caramelize, 1 to 2 minutes. Add the coconut milk, chicken broth, tamarind concentrate, and hoisin sauce. Reduce the heat to low and simmer the sauce until slightly thickened (look for a crème anglaise consistency), about 30 minutes. By that time, the natural oils from the peanuts should have surfaced. Turn off the heat and add the basil and cilantro. Cover and let cool. Store in the refrigerator for up to 3 days.

Chicken Broth: Put a 2-pound chicken (or 2 pounds meaty chicken bones) in a stockpot and add 5 quarts water. Add 6 lightly crushed scallions, ⅓ cup thinly sliced fresh ginger, and 1 pound peeled daikon cut into 2-inch-thick chunks. Bring to a boil over high heat. Reduce heat to low and simmer, partially covered, until reduced by about half, about 3 hours. If using commercial chicken stock, pick one that is labeled "no sodium" or "low sodium."

SWEET, SOUR, AND SPICY FISH SAUCE DRESSING

Makes about 2 cups

Sweet with sugar, sour with citrus juice, spicy with chilies, bitter with garlic, and salty with fish sauce, this condiment can be used as a dressing or as a dipping sauce. It is the ubiquitous condiment of Vietnam, served at every meal. It can be mild or bold depending on how you prepare the ingredients. Crushing the garlic and seeding the chilies will give you a relatively mild flavor. Slicing the garlic and seedless chilies will give you a slightly stronger flavor. Mincing the garlic and the chilies will give you a more pronounced flavor yet. Keeping the seeds in the chilies will intensify the flavor still more. The more the pungent garlic and chilies are broken down, the stronger the flavor of the sauce.

½ cup plus 2 tablespoons sugar

⅔ cup fish sauce

⅔ cup fresh lime or lemon juice

2 large garlic cloves, thinly sliced or minced

2 red Thai chilies, halved lengthwise, seeded (or not), and thinly sliced or minced

In a medium bowl, whisk together the sugar, fish sauce, and lime or lemon juice until the sugar is completely dissolved. Add the garlic and chilies. Let stand for 30 minutes before serving. Store in the refrigerator for up to 1 week.

NOTE: If you have fish sauce that is a little old but not black, use water to take the intensity of the saltiness down to a palatable level. Add 1 tablespoon of spring water at a time to the recipe, and keep tasting as you adjust.

SPICY VINEGAR DIPPING SAUCE

Makes about 2 cups

The ubiquitous "five-flavor-note" system—spicy, sweet, sour, salty, and bitter—is well represented in this dipping sauce. When you add a nutty sesame overtone, you have a winning combination for Korean-inspired Grilled Barely Marinated Beef (page 140), for which this dipping sauce was created; protein such as this recipe's marbled beef is rich, and the bold, vinegary characteristic of this dipping sauce is a perfectly refreshing match, breaking down the fat for easy digestion. This dipping sauce is also wonderful with any soy-marinated proteins, including grilled meat, seafood, or vegetables.

1 cup rice vinegar

½ cup thin soy sauce

¼ cup sugar

2 teaspoons dark sesame oil

1 to 1½ tablespoons finely grated fresh ginger

2 large garlic cloves, minced

2 scallions, trimmed and minced (white and green parts)

1 to 2 teaspoons Korean red chili powder or cayenne pepper

2 teaspoons sesame seeds, toasted (see page 25)

In a bowl, whisk together the rice vinegar, soy sauce, and sugar until the sugar is completely dissolved. Add the sesame oil, ginger, garlic, scallions, and chili powder and let steep for at least 1 hour. Pour some sauce into individual sauce dishes and garnish each serving with a sprinkle of toasted sesame seeds. This sauce can be made ahead of time and lasts about 1 week refrigerated.

CHINESE BLACK BEAN SAUCE

Makes about 1½ cups

I love black bean sauce. Pungent with fermented beans, garlic, ginger, and rice wine, it gives seafood, especially, a wonderful nutty and mildly spicy flavor. While there is a jarred version of this sauce, the homemade version is best. It offers a wonderful chunky texture that commercially made versions lack.

1   cup fermented black beans

2   tablespoons vegetable oil

3   large garlic cloves, crushed and minced

1 to 1½ tablespoons minced fresh ginger

½   cup Shaoxing rice wine or sake

2   teaspoons sugar

1. In a bowl, soak the black beans in water to cover for 20 minutes to get rid of the excess salt. Drain.

2. In a saucepan, heat the oil over medium heat. Stir-fry the garlic and ginger until golden, about 3 minutes. Add the black beans and stir-fry until fragrant, about 2 minutes. Reduce the heat to low, add the rice wine and sugar, and simmer until the liquid is reduced by half, about 10 minutes. Transfer the black bean sauce to a heatproof jar. Let cool, close, and refrigerate for up to 1 week.

MINTY SILKEN TOFU DIP

Makes about 2 cups

Silken tofu is perfect for making dips, because it is, as the name suggests, silky in texture. Combined with herbs and lightly chilled before serving, it is a refreshing complement to meat dishes. On the day I created this recipe, I wanted to serve it with lamb, so I picked fresh mint as the herb. I also used lemon juice, which added a slight tangy note and counterbalanced any fat the lamb might have had. Both mint and lemon also added a refreshing note to the tofu, and the black pepper gave it a mild sharp finishing note. Blended to the consistency of a fruit smoothie, it is delicious with Slow-Cooked Leg of Lamb (page 133). I'm not accustomed to eating mint jelly with lamb as some of my friends are—it is not common in French or Chinese cooking. I have always been intrigued with the combination, however, and it is what gave me the idea for this little culinary adventure.

One 14-ounce container medium-firm silken tofu

24   medium-to-large fresh mint leaves

Juice of 1 lemon

1   teaspoon kosher salt

½   teaspoon freshly ground black pepper

In a mini processor, blend the tofu, mint, lemon juice, salt, and pepper to a smooth consistency. Refrigerate until chilled before serving. Best made fresh.

GINGER AND SCALLION SALT DIP

**Makes about 1 cup
enough for 4 to 6 people**

⅓ cup finely grated fresh
young ginger

12 scallions, trimmed and minced
(white and green parts)

1 tablespoon kosher salt

⅓ cup vegetable oil

Of all the combinations of ginger and scallions in Asian cooking, this is one of the most interesting. The ingredients are cured in salt, which deepens and smooths their flavor. Oil is added to the dip, enhancing the texture. Quick and simple to make, it is also a perfect last-minute seasoning to any grilled meat or seafood, refreshing the palate as well. Earthy, spicy, and salty, it is best when made fresh.

Serve the dip with chicken—poached, steamed, grilled, roasted, or panfried—as is the tradition in Vietnamese or Chinese restaurants. This gingery dip is also excellent with shrimp, lobster, or grilled fish. Steamed rice is the perfect accompaniment "canvas" for dishes served with this wonderful dip. It allows fresh, clean flavors to come together on the palate without masking. Serve grilled bok choy as a vegetable side.

This dip is salty, and it is supposed to be. Just a small dab on any grilled meat or seafood will go a long way.

In a bowl, stir together the ginger, scallions, salt, and oil until well combined. Use immediately, or cover and refrigerate for up to 1 week.

THAI BASIL AND LEMON RELISH

Makes about 1 cup

4 lemons, peeled and segmented
(see note)

¼ cup sugar

1 large garlic clove, minced

1 small red Thai chili, stemmed,
seeded, and minced

¼ cup packed fresh Thai basil
leaves, minced

Thai basil has a flavor reminiscent of licorice and lemon. Combined with peeled and crushed lemon segments, its fragrance intensifies as the curing brings out the leaves' essential oils. Sweet with sugar and spicy with chilies, this sauce is perfect for seafood dishes such as Fish Patties (page 113). It is also wonderful with grilled prawns, frogs' legs, or fish fillets.

In a small bowl, crush the lemon segments with a fork to release the juice. Add the sugar and stir vigorously until the sugar is completely dissolved. Stir in the garlic, chili, and basil until evenly distributed. Let stand for 30 minutes prior to serving to allow the flavors to blend. Make this sauce fresh each time.

NOTE: To peel and segment citrus, slice the stem end off and stand the fruit, cut side down, on a cutting board. With a knife, starting at the top and slicing downward, cut off the peel down to the flesh. Hold the fruit in your hand and carefully cut on either side of each membrane to release each segment.

PINEAPPLE AND ONION CHUTNEY

Makes about 4 cups

Chutney (from the Indian word *chatni*) is an Indian-style relish traditionally made with fruit, vinegar, and any number of spices. This pineapple variation was an experiment involving a leftover and very ripe pineapple. A new sort of pan-Asian hybrid resulted. This chutney is an extraordinary complement to grilled beef, especially Garlic-Pepper Marinated Hanger Steak (page 136). Served with baby salad greens tossed with a Miso Salad Dressing (page 39) and some rice on the side, it transforms a relatively inexpensive cut of beef into a refreshing, exotic summer meal. This recipe is best made a day ahead of time, allowing the flavors to develop fully.

¼ cup vegetable oil

1 large red onion, halved and thinly sliced into half circles

3 to 4 tablespoons finely grated fresh ginger

1 large garlic clove, minced

1 large ripe pineapple, peeled, cored, and finely chopped

1 teaspoon Indian curry powder

Grated zest and juice of 1 lemon

Kosher salt and freshly ground black pepper to taste

3 tablespoons minced fresh mint

In a medium saucepan, heat the oil over medium-high heat. Add the onion, ginger, and garlic and sauté until golden, about 10 minutes. Add the pineapple and continue to cook until browned, 20 to 30 minutes. Add the curry powder, lemon zest, and lemon juice. Stir to distribute evenly. Season with salt and pepper and cook until thickened, about 10 minutes. Stir in 2 tablespoons of the mint, cook another minute or so, and remove from the heat. Transfer to a serving dish and garnish with the remaining mint before serving.

FRESH TOMATO CHUTNEY

Makes about 3 cups

Summer is when I crave the many varieties of wonderful, ripe tomatoes. I love to have them raw, with a bit of salt. But, loaded with natural sweetness at the peak of the season, tomatoes are delicious with just about anything. Use them in this recipe, a tomato relish that is sweet, tart, and spicy. Diced, the tomatoes are macerated in tangy rice vinegar and tamarind, sweetened just lightly with sugar, and spiced with Spice Route Blend. The chutney's mild heat and bitter flavor notes come from a combination of garlic, chilies, and ginger. Cilantro gives it a refreshing herbal, lemony note on the finish. While delicious freshly made, this recipe is best made a day ahead of time, allowing the flavors to develop fully.

4   large ripe tomatoes, peeled and seeded (see note)

2   tablespoons packed fresh cilantro leaves, minced

1   tablespoon rice vinegar

1   tablespoon palm sugar or granulated sugar

¼   cup Tamarind Concentrate (page 55)

¼   teaspoon Spice Route Blend (page 53)

1   tablespoon vegetable oil

1   small yellow onion, diced

1   large garlic clove, minced

1 to 1½ tablespoons finely grated fresh ginger

2   red Thai chilies, stemmed, seeded, and minced

1. Chop the tomatoes into ¾-inch dice. Transfer the tomatoes, along with the cilantro, to a bowl and set aside.

2. In another bowl, whisk together the rice vinegar and sugar until the sugar is completely dissolved. Stir in the tamarind concentrate and spice blend.

3. In a skillet, heat the oil over medium heat. Add the onion and stir-fry until golden, about 7 minutes. Add the garlic and stir-fry until just golden, about 5 minutes more. Add the ginger and Thai chilies and stir-fry until fragrant, 1 minute. Add the rice vinegar mixture and stir until just bubbling. Pour the sauce over the tomatoes and cilantro and stir well. Let cool completely, then refrigerate for up to 24 hours.

NOTE: To peel and seed tomatoes, use a paring knife to cut an X on the bottom of each tomato. Blanch each tomato in a pot of boiling water to loosen the skin, about 10 seconds. Peel the tomatoes and cut in half crosswise. Squeeze each tomato half to remove the seeds.

CUCUMBER AND PRESERVED LEMON YOGURT

Makes about 2 cups

Savory yogurts are especially delicious with spicy foods, because dairy tends to neutralize the heat, rendering the dishes milder, more palatable, and easier to digest. Whether you are grilling spicy or mild dishes, however, this cucumber and preserved lemon yogurt will be a hit. For a relatively simple recipe, the concoction yields a lot of flavor: the trick is the blending of mildly spicy garlic, rich yogurt, earthy cucumber and scallions, and slightly bitter preserved lemons. Like savory yogurts, preserved lemons or limes can be found in many food cultures throughout Asia. Once stirred with the juicy cucumber, rich and creamy Greek yogurt loosens up without ever becoming watery, which is a key consideration in a good sauce.

2   English (hothouse) cucumbers, peeled, seeded, and finely grated (about ⅔ cup)

1   cup plain Greek yogurt

1   large garlic clove, minced

1   tablespoon minced Preserved Lemons (page 55)

1   scallion, trimmed and minced (white and green parts)

Kosher salt and freshly ground black pepper to taste

1. Place the grated cucumbers in a fine-mesh sieve set over a bowl and let drain completely, about 1 hour. Press the pulp gently against the side of the sieve with the back of a large spoon. (Reserve the collected cucumber juice for Cucumber Lemonade, page 160, or sip it while you cook.)

2. In a small bowl, stir together the cucumber pulp, yogurt, garlic, lemon, and scallion until well combined. Season with salt and pepper. Best made fresh the day you serve it. Refrigerate until ready to serve.

SWEET AND SOUR CHILI AND BEAN PASTE

Makes about 1⅓ cups

You could call this recipe Asian ketchup. While its base is chilies and beans rather than tomatoes, the dipping sauce is boldly sweet and sour, and deep red in color. This sauce, however, packs a bit of heat. The vinegar and honey tame it, giving it a smooth, velvety texture and a distinctive and balanced flavor, and making it ideal for spreading on Asian wraps. A small amount goes a long way, although I have seen people gobble it up like ice cream. Serve with Grilled Barely Marinated Beef (page 140) and in combination with Spicy Vinegar Dipping Sauce (page 43).

¾ cup Korean hot bean paste

⅓ cup honey

¼ cup rice vinegar

In a bowl, whisk together the hot bean paste, honey, and rice vinegar until thoroughly combined. Transfer to a jar, cover, and refrigerate for up to 1 week.

LEMONGRASS AND GARLIC PASTE

Makes about ½ cup

This herb paste is used in many parts of Asia, so much so that many cooks, like my Aunt Loan, who now lives in Paris, keep a batch in the refrigerator and replenish it week after week. If you are a busy person, freeze the lemongrass and garlic paste in an ice cube tray and thaw only what you need. I use a fine grater to process both ingredients. It is important to break down the tough fibers of the lemongrass to make it palatable. It is also very important to grate the garlic to release its natural juices. The fish sauce and palm sugar are preserving agents.

¼ cup fish sauce

¼ cup palm sugar or granulated sugar

4 lemongrass stalks, trimmed, peeled, and finely grated (white and light green parts)

4 large garlic cloves, finely grated

In a bowl, mix together the fish sauce and sugar until the sugar is completely dissolved. Add the lemongrass and garlic and mix. To store, refrigerate for up to 1 week, or freeze in an ice cube tray for up to 3 months, covered.

NOTE: This paste is sufficient for 2 pounds of sliced beef, pork, or chicken, or whole shrimp or squid. Marinate for 30 minutes prior to grilling.

GINGER-GARLIC CHILI PASTE

Makes about 1 cup

There are many chili sauces available, smooth to coarse, bottled and jarred. Some are vinegary, others are salty, and still others are sweet. This chili paste is hot, sour, and salty, with ginger and garlic flavor notes. Ginger is considered a cure-all and is often used in combination with seafood in Asian cuisine. Garlic is known for cutting cholesterol and so is ideal when eating meats. While recipe testing, I was looking for a chili paste that was a bit different, complementing seafood and meats equally. This is what I came up with.

1½ cups red Thai chilies, stemmed and coarsely chopped

3 large garlic cloves, minced

3 tablespoons minced fresh ginger

3 tablespoons rice vinegar

1 teaspoon kosher salt

In a mini food processor, process the chilies, garlic, ginger, rice vinegar, and salt to a paste consistency. Cover and refrigerate for up to 3 weeks.

Variations
For a sweet chili paste, add 1 tablespoon simple syrup (see note, page 160) or palm sugar to the mini food processor along with the other ingredients.

To fry this chili paste, substitute vegetable oil for the vinegar and stir-fry the ingredients over medium heat until fragrant and a shade darker, about 7 minutes. Cover and refrigerate for up to 1 week.

NOTE: For a milder sauce, seed the chilies.

Opposite (top to bottom): Preserved Lemons (page 55), Ginger-Garlic Chili Paste, and Ginger and Scallion Salt Dip (page 45)

YELLOW SPICE PASTE

Makes about 1⅔ cups

Spice pastes are popular in Asia. They explode in your mouth with refreshing herbal notes and bold dried spices. I love spice pastes because they taste of the earth and offer so many flavor notes that they inevitably prompt conversations at table with guests trying to guess the ingredients. "What is in this?" is the question that keeps coming up as they enjoy the flavor layering. This yellow spicy paste is extremely versatile: made with just about equal parts dried spices and fresh herbs, it can be used to further enhance a liquid marinade or a yogurt marinade, or it can be used as is to marinate meats or seafood, as in the Spiced Yogurt Lamb Kebobs (page 135) or Fish Patties (page 113). There is enough here for several recipes. Sometimes spice pastes are also used for stir-frying or adding to braised dishes, turning something simple into something quite spectacular. Asian herbal–spice pastes may not do it all, but they surely can do a lot.

- 2   tablespoons palm sugar
- 1   tablespoon ground coriander
- 1   teaspoon ground nutmeg
- 1   teaspoon ground turmeric
- 7   red Thai chilies, stemmed, seeded, and minced
- 4   large garlic cloves, grated
- 3   large shallots, grated
- 3   large fresh kaffir lime leaves, minced
- 2   lemongrass stalks, trimmed, peeled, and finely grated (white and light green parts)
- ¼   cup unsalted roasted macadamia nuts, ground to a powder
- 1 to 1½ tablespoons finely grated fresh galangal
- 1 to 1½ tablespoons finely grated fresh ginger
- ½   cup Tamarind Concentrate (page 55)
- ¼   cup vegetable oil
- 1   tablespoon shrimp paste

1. In a bowl, whisk together the palm sugar, coriander, nutmeg, and turmeric. Add the chilies, garlic, shallots, kaffir lime leaves, lemongrass, nuts, galangal, ginger, and tamarind concentrate and mix. Set aside.

2. In a saucepan, heat the oil over medium heat and stir-fry the shrimp paste until one shade darker, about 5 minutes. Add the spice mixture and continue to stir-fry until well combined and darker by two shades but not burned, 10 minutes more. Transfer the paste, including all of the oil, to a heat-proof jar. To store, cover and refrigerate for up to 1 week.

SPICE ROUTE BLEND

Makes ¾ cup

⅓ cup coriander seeds

2 small dried lemons (see page 21), crushed

3 tablespoons cumin seeds

2 tablespoons green cardamom pods

1 teaspoon whole cloves

1 teaspoon black peppercorns

1 teaspoon ground nutmeg

1 teaspoon ground turmeric

½ teaspoon ground cinnamon

I named this spice blend after the legendary spice routes of Asia that Marco Polo traveled. Links between China, Central Asia, and the West, the spice routes were not only about mercantile trade, they were avenues for culinary exchange. For example, Egyptian flat breads made their way into Chinese kitchens, and Persian noodles spread throughout Europe and Asia. This Spice Route Blend is derived from the pungent Indian garam masala spice mix. The only ingredient in this blend you might have trouble finding is the dried lemons, but do not let that stop you. Either omit them, or make your own.

In a spice grinder, grind together the coriander, lemons, cumin, cardamom, cloves, and peppercorns to a fine powder. Transfer to a small bowl and stir in the nutmeg, turmeric, and cinnamon until well combined. Store in an airtight jar in a dark, cool place for up to 1 year.

NOTE: If you do not think that you will be using all of the spice blend within a year, halve the recipe.

PEPPERY, SWEET, AND SAVORY FIVE-SPICE BLEND

Makes about ¼ cup

2 tablespoons kosher salt

1 tablespoon Chinese five-spice powder

1 tablespoon sugar

1 teaspoon freshly ground black pepper

This dry rub gives meat a curious-but-oh-so-delicious licorice-like flavor. In China, this blend is often used to season chicken legs, which are then deep-fried. I like to grill chicken legs during the summer for a lighter version of the classic. I prefer to use the sweet and juicy dark meat of the legs because its richness holds up to the pungent dry rub. The milder white meat works, too, especially for those who prefer a more healthful cut of meat. Just make sure the breast does not dry out while cooking. As a last-minute table seasoning, this salty spice mix is also wonderful with stronger meats like duck and lamb. Only a small dab is necessary. You can even turn grilled steak into something extraordinary by sprinkling each bite lightly with the five-spice blend, mimicking what the French do with their sel de Guérande: season to taste as you go.

In a small bowl, mix together the salt, five-spice powder, sugar, and pepper until well combined. Store in an airtight jar in a dark, cool place for up to one year.

TOASTED RICE FLOUR

Makes about 2 cups

Toasted rice flour adds a nutty flavor to dishes. In Asia, it is often used as a binder or to dust on food items prior to cooking. While you can buy it, in my opinion homemade tastes better. You can also use it instead of bread crumbs. For example, panfried fish or fried chicken is especially delicious when dusted with seasoned toasted rice flour.

2　cups short- or medium-grain sushi rice

In a dry skillet over medium heat, toast the rice, constantly shaking the pan so as not to burn the rice, until deep golden in color, about 10 minutes. Pour the rice into a bowl and let cool. In a spice grinder, process the rice to a fine powder. Sift through a fine-mesh sieve set over a bowl. Transfer any remaining broken grains into the spice grinder and repeat the process until all of the rice powder can be sifted. Store in an airtight jar in the refrigerator for up to 1 year.

PICKLED GINGER

Makes about 1 cup ginger without the pickling liquid

Young, juicy ginger is used to make this lightly pickled condiment, which is used as a palate cleanser and side dish to all sorts of grilled foods. Store–bought pickled ginger is fine, but it often has food coloring and is not very distinguished in flavor. The fresh–made type is really delicious, with deep and subtle flavor notes, and it requires only five basic ingredients: ginger, salt, rice vinegar, water and sugar. With very little effort, you can have terrific pickled ginger within a week.

1　pound fresh young ginger, peeled and broken into its natural knobs

2　teaspoons kosher salt

1½ cups rice vinegar

½　cup spring or filtered water, boiled and cooled

¼　cup sugar

1. Put the ginger in a bowl and sprinkle with the salt. Toss. Cover and refrigerate for 24 hours.

2. In a bowl, whisk together the rice vinegar, water, and sugar until the sugar is completely dissolved. Set aside.

3. Blot each ginger knob dry with a paper towel. Slice each knob paper-thin (you should be able to see through each slice). Put the slices in a jar and pour the vinegar mixture on top. Cover and refrigerate for 1 to 2 weeks prior to serving.

PRESERVED LEMONS

Makes 1 quart

This is one of those instances where a foodstuff gets better with age: the longer the lemons sit in the salted juice used as a preserving base, the more they give up their own sour natural juices. Eventually, the rinds become very soft, the fruit having almost dissolved, yielding a chunky paste of amazing salty and sour juices.

16 lemons, preferably organic, scrubbed and halved

1 tablespoon kosher salt

Juice 16 lemon halves and reserve the rest. Transfer the reserved lemon halves to a quart jar, crushing them and sprinkling them with the salt in the process. Pour the lemon juice on top. Shake the jar and refrigerate for at least 1 year before using, shaking the jar daily to coat the lemons with their juices. Each month, push the softened lemons down with a wooden spoon. Eventually, the lemon halves will give up their juices and the pulpy halves will be submerged in their own juices. Keeps for up to 3 years.

TAMARIND CONCENTRATE

Makes about 2 cups

Tamarind is widely used as a souring agent in many of Asia's food cultures, including those of Thailand, Vietnam, Cambodia, and India. It provides a tangy note to soups and sauces without the sharp, sour edge of lemons or limes. Tamarind, while sour in character, has a faintly sweet background note, which balances out its tanginess. While you can occasionally find fresh tamarind pods in markets, the packaged pulp is more common. Tamarind concentrate is available commercially, but it is not as good as the homemade version.

One 16-ounce package tamarind pulp, cut into 8 equal pieces

2 cups boiling water

Put the tamarind pulp in a medium bowl and pour the water over it. Cover with a plate and allow the pulp to steam and soften, about 30 minutes. With a fork, loosen the pulp in the hot water until thick and cloudy. Strain through a sieve set over a bowl, pressing on the pulp with the back of a large spoon. Discard the seeds and fibers. Transfer the concentrate to a jar. Cover and refrigerate for up to 1 week, or freeze in an ice cube tray for up to 3 months.

CHAPTER 4 | FLAT BREADS, RICE, AND NOODLES

You might wonder what rice is doing in a grill book—obviously you don't grill it. You can serve it with just about anything you do grill, however, and that is our point of entry.

When putting a meal together, consider the starch as a sort of canvas for highlighting all sorts of colorful side dishes. A simple bowl of steamed rice is a perfect accompaniment to any of the protein and vegetable recipes in this book.

Rice is not the only starch that works with Asian flavors, however. Potatoes, yams, sweet potatoes, and taro root (see chapter 5 "Vegetables and Fruits") are all terrific backgrounds for spicy and complex grilled foods. (They are often used to mediate the intense flavors of hot curries.) Other starches that work beautifully as accompaniments for spicy grilled foods include noodles and flat breads.

While I have included a recipe for steamed rice (there is a bit of an art to it), I also have other simple rice recipes that are a bit more exotic, including herbal sticky rice infused with its bamboo leaf wrapping. Another favorite among my guests is the Japanese sushi rice pocket—essentially rice in little golden fried tofu pockets. Here, short- to medium-grain rice is boiled in water, then, when fully cooked, transferred to a large wooden platter. It is then fanned out on the platter to cool to room temperature, and simultaneously drizzled with a sweetened pickling liquid. This is a traditional Japanese rice preparation technique, often specifically employed with sushi. The technique keeps the rice from spoiling when kept at room temperature for an extended period, and the vinegar acts as a preservative for raw fish.

If you think of noodles as something uniformly bland and uninteresting, you are in for a wonderful surprise. There are more Asian noodle types than you can imagine, and when drizzled with dipping sauces, they are transformed into fabulously flavorful side dishes. The key here is understanding which noodles work with what, and which sauces enhance best. Some of the simplest and most delicious noodle dishes are included in this chapter.

Many Asian cultures, especially those in the south, consider noodles a snack and rarely serve them at meals. Noodle types include mung bean and potato-starch cellophane, rice, wheat, egg, and buckwheat (with green tea and pink plum variations), and many of these have several thin-to-thick variations. These flavorful noodles complement grilled meats and vegetables perfectly.

Many people are surprised to learn that a number of flat breads are widely used in Asian cultures and that they can be a wonderful part of any grilled protein meal. These include scallion pancakes, flaky Indian-inspired parathas, and the delicate wraps served with Peking duck, to name a few. They can be torn and dipped in a dipping sauce, or used to wrap any grilled meat, seafood, or vegetable.

One of my favorite flat breads is the classic northern Chinese scallion spiral bread (pancake). It is shallow-fried in a wok until puffy and crispy, loaded with delicious pungent scallions, and seasoned with salt and sesame oil. For this book, I have revisited the classic and created a true flat bread that is rolled out until super thin and cooked in a dry skillet or grilled. This bread becomes flexible, much like a Mexican flour tortilla. It still includes the pungent sesame, scallion, and salt flavors but is much lighter because it is not fried.

SCALLION FLAT BREADS

Makes 12

Based on the traditional fried northern Chinese scallion pancakes, these thin, flaky flat breads are delicious torn and dipped in yogurt, or used to wrap grilled meats. They are also less oily than the classic version, and require less prep time.

These are best freshly cooked. The longer they sit, the harder they get, just like most breads. That said, if you are having a party and you want to make them ahead of time, be sure to wrap them in plastic wrap after they are cooked. To reheat, steam them for 30 seconds. Steaming bread is a common Chinese cooking technique. The process gets rid of any dry flour remaining on the bread from rolling it out. It also renders the once crisp flat bread more elastic.

3   cups all-purpose flour

2   teaspoons kosher salt

2   teaspoons baking powder

6   scallions, trimmed and finely sliced (white and light green parts)

1   cup spring or filtered water

2   tablespoons vegetable oil

1   tablespoon dark sesame oil

1. Sift 2 cups of the flour, the salt, and baking powder together into a large bowl. Add the scallions and stir to blend. Make a well in the center and add the water and the vegetable and sesame oils. Work the flour in toward the center with a spoon to incorporate the dry and wet ingredients. Turn the soft dough out onto a floured work surface and knead, using some or all of the remaining 1 cup flour, until smooth and elastic, about 5 minutes. Wrap in plastic and allow to rest 30 minutes at room temperature.

2. Cut the dough into 12 equal pieces. Form into balls, then flatten and roll out into 8-inch disks.

3. Heat a large skillet over medium heat. Oil lightly and cook the disks until lightly golden, 1 to 2 minutes per side. (When the disks begin to form bubbles here and there, it's time to flip.) Serve hot.

NOTE: To reheat the breads, fill a wok half-full with water and bring to a boil over high heat. Wrap the breads in a kitchen towel (open side up) and place on a plate that fits on a bamboo steamer rack. There must be enough space between the plate and the sides of the steamer to allow the steam to circulate. Cover the rack and place on top of the wok of rapidly simmering water. Steam for 30 seconds to 1 minute.

DELICATE SESAME WRAPS

Makes 24

These super-thin wraps have a light, chewy texture to them, unlike scallion flat breads, which are flaky. They are traditionally used for wrapping Peking duck or for moo shoo pork. Easy to make, the dish is essentially flour that is precooked with boiling water prior to kneading. This precooking technique makes for great elasticity in the finished food. The wraps are cooked in a dry pan, two at a time over low heat, then pulled apart prior to serving alongside all sorts of foods, including meats and vegetables. They are best when just made, although they may be reheated (see note).

1 cup spring or filtered water

3 cups all-purpose flour

Dark sesame oil for brushing

1. In a small saucepan, bring the water to a boil over high heat. Meanwhile, sift 2 cups of the flour into a large bowl and make a well in the center. Add the boiling water and work the flour in toward the center with a spoon to incorporate the dry and wet ingredients. (You must work fast, as the hot water will precook the flour, making it more elastic in the process. If you are unable to work the hot dough with your hands, use a mixer with a dough hook.) Turn the dough out onto a floured work surface and knead, using some or all of the remaining flour, until smooth and elastic, about 5 minutes.

2. Shape the dough into a cylinder and cut it into 24 equal pieces. Shape each into a ball and flatten once on a clean work surface with the palm of your hand. Brush the top side of each round of dough generously and all the way to the edge with sesame oil. Take 2 rounds of dough, oiled sides facing each other, and press them together. Repeat to make 12 pairs of dough. Wrap in plastic and allow to rest 30 minutes at room temperature.

3. Roll out each pair of dough rounds into a very thin disk about 8 inches in diameter.

4. Heat a pan over medium heat. Oil lightly and cook the disks for about 1 minute per side. (When the disks begin to puff up and turn white with a few golden spots, it's time to flip.) While still warm, find the seam and carefully pull each wrap apart into two halves. You should have 24 wraps total. Serve at once to wrap all sorts of grilled foods.

NOTE: To reheat the wraps, fill a wok half-full with water and bring to a boil over high heat. Stack the wraps, enclosed in a kitchen towel (open side up), on a plate that fits on a bamboo steamer rack. There must be enough space between the plate and the sides of the steamer to allow the steam to circulate. Cover the rack and place on top of the wok. Steam for about 30 seconds.

PARATHAS (ROTIS)

Makes 12

3   cups all-purpose flour, plus more for kneading and rolling

1   tablespoon baking powder

1   teaspoon kosher salt

1½ cups spring or filtered water

½   cup vegetable oil or ghee

I learned this recipe from one of my assistants while teaching at the Institute of Culinary Education (ICE) in New York City. Born in Guyana of Indian parents, she asked if she could make her family's version of a special, flaky flat bread called paratha (and somewhat interchangeably, roti). I said sure and invited the students to watch as she started by creating handmade dough. Barely kneaded, the dough—which, unlike the original Indian version, has baking powder—was lumpy and moist. When rolled into a flat disk, it became elastic. She brushed oil all over the top, mentioning that ghee would also work perfectly. From there she went into a near balletic series of hand motions. Finally, the dough was rolled into a thin (and now more pliable) disk and pan-cooked until just golden. The little bread was so beautiful; the whole class was ready to dig in at this point. And then came the real surprise. She suddenly took the flat bread from the pan and smacked it around in a towel, fluffing it up! "You have to beat the hell out of it," she exclaimed, further explaining that the technique would render the warm bread super-light and flaky. It was, we all agreed, the best flatbread we had ever had. Note that you can cook this bread in a pan on a stove top or directly on your grill. This bread is the perfect accompaniment for chutneys or for getting that last bit of sauce off your plate.

1. Sift the flour, baking powder, and salt together into a large bowl. Make a well in the center. Add the water in the well and gradually incorporate the dry ingredients into the water. Turn out the dough onto a floured work surface, and knead for a couple of minutes. Shape into a ball, lightly flour, and let rest for 30 minutes, covered in plastic wrap.

2. On a clean work surface lightly dusted with flour, roll out a dough ball into a ¹⁄₁₆-inch-thick disk. Brush oil or ghee all over the top side. Make a single straight incision from the center to the edge. Lift the dough at the incision and roll it back onto itself until you have a layered cone. Hold the cone, pointy side down, with one hand. Using the thumb of your other hand, push the layered edges of the dough into the center of the cone until you have a ball. Repeat this process with the remaining 11 pieces of dough. When done, cover the dough balls with a clean, damp kitchen towel and allow them to rest for 30 minutes to 1 hour at room temperature.

3. On a lightly floured work surface, flatten a dough ball with your palm and roll it out into a ¹⁄₁₆-inch-thick disk. (You will notice that the oil has now been well incorporated into the dough.)

4. Heat a large skillet over medium heat. Lightly oil and cook each disk until golden with occasional lightly blackened spots, about 2 minutes per side. Remove from the heat, wrap in a clean kitchen towel, and fluff by smacking your hands together with the bread in between. Serve at once.

OR

Prepare a medium-hot fire in a charcoal grill, or preheat a gas grill to 400°F (medium high). Place the roti on the grill until golden with grill marks. When puffy, flip and grill the other side, about 1 to 2 minutes per side. To eat, tear or fluff in towel.

NOTES: Classic Indian parathas do not contain baking powder. This recipe, which does include baking powder, is very common in Guyana, as is the use of vegetable oil instead of ghee.

Ghee, a clarified butter, can be purchased at Indian, Pakistani, and Bangladeshi stores and many natural foods stores.

You may have to sweep up bits of the paratha that fly out of the fluffing towel. This is a small price to pay, given the wonderful flavor of the bread.

SUSHI RICE IN FRIED TOFU POCKETS

Serves 6 to 8

These little golden-fried tofu pockets filled with mildly sweet and sour sushi rice are easy to eat with your fingers. The white rice is speckled with contrasting colors of yellow pickled daikon, orange burdock, or pink ginger, and makes for a wonderful presentation. The salty, sweet, and sometimes vinegary pickle garnishes are available at Japanese or Korean markets. They give the rice just enough flavor and crunchy texture to make it a conversation piece at the table. The golden tofu pocket holds everything together, adding elegance to an otherwise humble dish. Fried tofu pockets are available in Japanese markets, and usually come in packages of ten. Each is then cut in half, thus creating two pockets ready to be filled.

- 2 cups short- or medium-grain white or brown sushi rice, rinsed once
- 2 cups spring or filtered water
- 2 tablespoons rice vinegar, plus more for forming rice
- 2 teaspoons sugar
- 2 tablespoons drained sliced pickled ginger, daikon, or burdock, minced
- 10 square fried tofu pockets, halved crosswise

  Seaweed flakes (nori) for garnish

1. In a medium pot, combine the rice and water. Stir to level. Cover the pot, cook over medium-low heat until the rice has absorbed all of the water, about 20 minutes. Turn off the heat and fluff the rice with a spoon. Allow to rest, covered, for 10 minutes.

2. Meanwhile, in a small bowl, whisk together the 2 tablespoons rice vinegar and sugar until the sugar is completely dissolved.

3. Transfer the cooked rice to a Japanese round wooden rice container and spread it out in a thin layer. While fanning (using a traditional bamboo paddle, hand-held paper fan, a card, or anything that works) the rice to cool, work in the vinegar mixture and pickled ginger, daikon, or burdock.

4. Moisten your hands with rice vinegar to keep the rice from sticking to them. Divide the rice into 20 equal portions. Shape each portion into an oblong piece and fit snugly into a tofu pocket half to make 20 rice-filled tofu pockets. Sprinkle lightly with seaweed flakes before serving.

NOTE: It is important to fan the rice while working in the vinegar mixture. This ensures that the rice stays firm and moist as you introduce the liquid.

HERBAL STICKY RICE IN BAMBOO LEAVES

Serves 8

Sticky rice can serve beautifully as a base and binder in sweet leaf-wrapped foods. This bundle is slightly savory, however, and will surprise and delight your guests while adding an exotic visual note to the table. The bamboo leaves add a bittersweet note that permeates the wrap, and simmering the encased rice for 1 to 2 hours allows the flavor of the leaves to penetrate the soft, ever-more broken-down and tender rice. This leaf-wrapped rice is a great complement and a perfectly appropriate "blank canvas" for many of the marinated proteins in this book, but it is especially wonderful with Five-Spice Marinated Duck (page 125) and a side of Pickled Daikon, Carrot, and Cucumber (page 76).

2   cups short-grain white
    sticky rice

½   cup yellow mung beans

2   tablespoons vegetable oil

1 to 1½ tablespoons minced fresh
    ginger

2   large garlic cloves, minced

2   scallions, trimmed and sliced
    into ¼-inch-thick rounds (white
    and green parts)

1   bunch fresh cilantro, root ends
    removed, leaves and tender
    stems finely chopped

6   medium dried shiitakes, soaked
    in water until soft, drained,
    stems removed, and chopped

8   cups chicken broth (page 41)
    or water

16 dried bamboo leaves, soaked
    until soft, about 30 minutes

1. In a large bowl, mix together the sticky rice and mung beans, add 4 cups water and soak at least 4 hours, or cover and refrigerate overnight. Drain and set aside.

2. Heat the oil in a saucepan over medium heat. Stir-fry the ginger, garlic, and scallions until golden, 10 to 15 minutes. Add the cilantro and stir-fry until wilted, about 1 minute. Add the herbal mixture and shiitakes to the rice and mung beans, stirring well to distribute evenly.

3. Bring the broth or water to a boil in a stockpot over high heat. Meanwhile, make the rice bundle: Overlap 2 long, slender bamboo leaves lengthwise by 1½ to 2 inches (the edge of one leaf will meet the central rib of the other). Place 2 heaping tablespoons of the rice mixture, shaping the rice into a 1½-by-4-inch rectangle, in the center and along the length of the leaves. Fold the side of the leaf closest to you over the rice. Fold in the opposite end toward the center. Fold in each pointy end toward the center and tie the rectangular bundle with kitchen string as you would a gift package. Repeat with the remaining leaves and rice mixture.

4. Place the stuffed bamboo leaves in the pot. Reduce the heat to a simmer, cover the pot, and cook for 1 to 2 hours. The longer you cook the rice, the softer and more fragrant it will be. Serve bamboo leaf–bundles for each diner to unwrap.

Variations

Replace the rice in the master recipe with either of the following kinds of rice.

Steamed Long-Grain Rice: Rinse 2 cups long-grain rice 3 times, until the water is only slightly cloudy. Add to a saucepan with 3 cups water and bring to a boil over medium heat. Cover, reduce the heat to medium-low, and simmer until cooked, about 25 minutes. Turn off the heat, fluff with a fork, and cover again. Let stand for 10 minutes before serving. Makes about 4 cups.

Herbal Steamed Long-Grain Rice: Prepare steamed rice (above) using chicken broth instead of water, but first, mix the stir-fried herbs from the master recipe into the rinsed rice. Then add the chicken broth, level the rice, and cook according to the instructions for steamed rice. If you are unable to find bamboo leaves for the master recipe, use this variation. The dish will be missing the smoky tealike flavor, but it will still be fragrant and delicious.

GREEN TEA AND PLUM SOBA MEDLEY

Serves 6 to 8

2 bundles green tea soba noodles

2 bundles pink plum soba noodles

¼ cup thin soy sauce

1 tablespoon dark sesame oil

2 tablespoons rice vinegar

Pickled ginger, drained, for garnish

Black sesame seeds for garnish

Soba are wonderfully subtle Japanese noodles made from buckwheat flour. In Japan, soba are sold in clear plastic packages containing three to eight individual bundles, each tied with a paper ribbon. When served freshly made in restaurants, they are often prepared with great flair by a trained soba noodle master, some-times in full view of diners. Served immediately—"from the soba master directly to your plate"—they are valued as a special dining ritual as well as a food. Whether fresh or dried, soba have a unique nutty flavor that perfectly complements a wide variety of Asian grilled protein recipes. The green tea version offers an unexpected mild bitter note. I like to mix subtly sweet and tangy pink plum soba with green tea soba for flavor and color contrast. Pickled ginger and a light sprinkle of black sesame seeds add flavor and enhance the presentation. Use soba to complement Sweet Miso-Marinated Fish (page 115) and Fresh Zucchini Salad (page 78).

1. In separate large pots of boiling water, cook each noodle type individually until tender yet firm, about 3 minutes. Drain and rinse under cold running water.

2. Meanwhile, in a bowl, whisk together the soy sauce, sesame oil, and rice vinegar. Add the noodles and toss until evenly coated. Divide among individual plates, gar-nish each serving with pickled ginger, and sprinkle lightly with black sesame seeds.

STIR-FRIED POTATO STARCH NOODLES WITH CARROTS, SHIITAKES, AND SPINACH

Serves 6 to 8

One 12-ounce package Korean potato starch noodles

3 tablespoons vegetable oil

1 large garlic clove, minced

2 carrots, peeled and julienned

8 medium-to-large fresh shiitake mushrooms, stemmed and julienned

2 scallions, trimmed and sliced into ¼-inch-thick rounds (white and light green parts)

4 tablespoons thin soy sauce

2 teaspoons dark sesame oil

½ teaspoon sugar

8 ounces baby spinach

Freshly ground black pepper to taste

Toasted sesame seeds for garnish (see page 25)

This savory noodle dish is all about texture and color, with slippery translucent noodles, crunchy bright orange carrots, slightly chewy brown shiitakes, and tender green spinach. Unlike many other noodle recipes, this dish can be made ahead of time and served at room temperature or lightly chilled without compromise to flavor or texture. Serve it with Grilled Barely Marinated Beef (page 140) or just about any soy-marinated meat or seafood in this book. Potato starch noodles are easily found in Asian food markets, particularly Korean and Japanese markets. In a pinch, you can use Chinese cellophane (bean thread) noodles, but the potato starch noodles are thicker, have more "tooth" to them, and are easier to cook.

If you do not have much experience cooking thin noodles, go slowly. The thinner Chinese cellophane noodles are easy to overcook—essentially, ruin—much like angel hair pasta.

1. Soak the noodles in water to cover until rehydrated and pliable, about 30 minutes. Drain. In a large pot of boiling water, cook for 3 minutes. Drain and rinse under cold running water. Drain again.

2. Heat 1 tablespoon of the vegetable oil in a skillet over high heat. Stir-fry the garlic until lightly golden, 2 to 3 minutes. Add the carrots and cook until just wilted, 1 to 2 minutes. Add the shiitakes, half the scallions, 1 tablespoon of the soy sauce, 1 teaspoon of the sesame oil, and the sugar and cook for 30 seconds. Add the spinach and stir-fry until just wilted, another 30 seconds. Transfer the stir-fry to a plate.

3. Add the remaining 2 tablespoons vegetable oil, 1 teaspoon sesame oil, and 3 tablespoons soy sauce to the skillet. Stir-fry the noodles until heated through, about 3 minutes. Return the vegetable stir-fry to the skillet, season with pepper, and using two forks, toss to distribute the ingredients evenly throughout the noodles. Transfer the noodles to a serving dish. Garnish with the remaining scallions, sprinkle lightly with sesame seeds, and serve warm, at room temperature, or lightly chilled.

RICE VERMICELLI WITH SCALLION OIL AND FRESH VEGETABLES

Serve 6 to 8

This combination of rice vermicelli drizzled with scallion oil, crunchy sliced cucumber, carrots, and tender lettuce leaves is the backbone for many Vietnamese grilled protein specialties. Known as a "table salad," when paired with grilled foods it creates a perfect balance of cooked versus raw ingredients. It is light and refreshing with mint, and nutty with fried scallion oil and crushed roasted peanuts. It also makes for a dramatic "at-table" presentation of white, green, orange, and golden colors. When preparing the table salad, arrange each ingredient individually (in its own pile) on a single plate for everyone to pick from, mimicking the classic Vietnamese family-style presentation. It is perfect with grilled meats and seafood such as Lemongrass and Kaffir Lime Leaf Marinated Pork Skewers (page 132), Grilled Beef in Grape Leaves (page 139), and Grilled Shrimp Sausages (page 102), to name a few.

1 12-ounce package dried rice vermicelli

¼ cup vegetable oil

3 scallions, trimmed and thinly sliced into rounds (white and green parts)

3 carrots, peeled and julienned

Leaves from 2 heads Boston or Bibb lettuce

2 unripe carambolas (star fruit), sliced paper-thin crosswise (optional)

1 English (hothouse) cucumber, peeled, halved lengthwise, seeded, and sliced paper-thin crosswise

1 bunch fresh mint sprigs

1 cup unsalted roasted peanuts, crushed

Grilled meat or seafood for serving

Sweet, Sour, and Spicy Fish Sauce Dressing (page 42) for serving

1. Put the rice vermicelli in a large bowl with water to cover. Let soak until pliable, about 30 minutes. In a large pot of boiling water, cook the vermicelli for no more than 5 seconds. Drain and rinse under cold running water. Transfer to a dish, cover with plastic, and set aside.

2. In a small saucepan, heat the oil over medium heat. Fry the scallions until fragrant and light golden, about 5 minutes. Remove from heat and let cool. Toss the rice vermicelli with the scallion oil (including the scallions) and transfer to a dish.

3. On a platter, arrange, in individual piles, the carrots, lettuce leaves, carambolas (if using), cucumber, and mint sprigs. Put the peanuts in a separate bowl. Instruct guests to take some vermicelli, carrots, cucumbers, carambolas, lettuce leaves (freshly torn), mint leaves (pinching off the stems and freshly torn), and toss in their individual dish (a large soup bowl or a deep plate is best) until the ingredients are evenly distributed. Place some grilled meat or seafood on top, sprinkle with peanuts, and drizzle with the sauce.

NOTE: You can also create a finger food using all the ingredients in this "table salad" as a wrap for grilled meat or seafood. Simply take a lettuce leaf and top with a small amount of rice vermicelli, cucumber, carrots, carambola slices (if using), and 1 or 2 mint leaves. Top with some grilled meat or seafood, sprinkle with peanuts, and wrap the lettuce leaf to enclose the ingredients. Dip this fresh spring roll in the sauce.

CHAPTER 5 | VEGETABLES AND FRUITS

This chapter covers grilled vegetables and fruits, including some starchy tubers that go particularly well with grilled meats and seafood. Salads and dressings are also included. I should note right at the beginning that I love vegetables more than any other food. "Eat your vegetables" was my childhood mantra, and I reveled in any leafy thing from my French grandmother's garden in Blois, even while pondering the possibility of something green from my Chinese grandmother's plot in Phnom Penh.

I have included a wide array of fruits and vegetables that are readily available in Western markets. Apples, bananas, pears, carrots, cabbage, onions, eggplant, and bell peppers—they all make a perfect starting point for Asian flavors on the grill. (They are all used in authentic Asian cooking, too.) I have also included some Asian and other specialty foods for fun, and because they are increasingly available in those same Western markets. Japanese eggplant, bok choy, Asian pears, and sunchokes (to name a few) fall into this category, and they make for memorable dishes and terrific variety in your menus. Herbs are also included here because some Asian food cultures (notably Vietnamese and Cambodian) use them the way Western cuisines use vegetables—as accompaniments to main dishes. Vegetarian dishes are also included, both for the devoted vegetarian and for those who like the occasional light dish, the low-calorie meal, or just a change of pace. Here you will also find tofu, which, like other soy-based foods, forms an important part of many Asian diets. For those who think of tofu as uninspiring mush, take heart. Asian cooks have been working with this ingredient for centuries, and believe me, they have done some pretty remarkable things with it. I share them with you here.

Whenever possible, try to use seasonal, locally grown, and organic fruits and vegetables for your grill menus. They have intense flavor notes and tend to be fresh. (Grilling will not save a food item that is past its prime—use it for soup instead.) Fruits and vegetables bring a wide variety of textures, flavors, and colors to your table. They lift and refresh the palate during a meal. As a general rule, I serve two to three vegetable dishes for every meat or seafood dish. (My husband, after returning from an excursion to a barbecue joint "down South," told me that this combination was also an American classic, appearing on many menus as "meat 'n' three.") I also make sure that a variety of colors are present so as to cover a wide vitamin and mineral spectrum. (This makes for a more appetizing, visually exciting plate, too.)

The techniques in this chapter vary from grilling to pickling, braising, and sautéing. Any and all of these can make for wonderful side dishes when grilling meats and seafoods. The variety of new flavors you can coax out of the most familiar vegetables by grilling them may surprise you, as in my sesame oil–infused grilled eggplant with sweet miso dipping sauce. It is part of a Grilled Vegetables medley (page 93). The idea of grilling fruits may also offer some new menu excursions for you, as in my Grilled Fruit combo (page 91).

Those of you who think of pickles as something in a jar that tastes of vinegar and dill will be in for a pleasant surprise. Asian pickling yields all sorts of light foods in a matter of minutes. These items are particularly refreshing during a meal, cleansing and reviving your palate as you go.

Braising simply refers to cooking a food in liquid over low heat for an extended period of time. The technique brings out the flavors in such foods as eggplant and sunchokes. Sautéing can often be done with a skillet right on the grill itself, and this approach works well for simple stir-fried Asian greens with garlic, such as bok choy, Chinese broccoli, or water spinach. And you will enjoy the experience of rediscovering something as simple as a carrot or cucumber when you julienne or very thinly slice it for a salad.

Vegetables provide a year-round changing menu. Summer is a time when you can select a wonderful array of fresh vegetables, but it need not be the only season for grilling them. Spring brings such specialty items as asparagus and cabbage, and these can be enjoyed grilled or tossed in a salad. A summertime meal is the perfect occasion for sweet and crisp vegetables eaten raw or very lightly cooked. Accordingly, I have provided a few salad recipes such as thinly sliced raw zucchini; Asian coleslaw with carrots, cabbage, and red onions; a spicy cucumber and red onion salad; and a sweet and tart mango salad. You will find a wonderful array of squashes in the fall, ranging from the familiar acorn and butternut squash to the somewhat more unusual dark green–skinned, deep orange–fleshed kabocha squash, also known as Japanese pumpkin. And frozen edamame are available all year long, so you can enjoy them during any season. Potatoes and other root vegetables are also available any time of the year, and are terrific as grilled accompaniments or "stand-alones," depending on your mood or menu.

PICKLED DAIKON, CARROT, AND CUCUMBER

Serves 6 to 8

Some authentic Chinese restaurants serve small dishes of pickled vegetables as starters, essentially to whet the appetite. Generally, these consist of sliced daikon, carrot, and cucumber. They are salted and drained initially to reduce their natural water content, preventing the dilution of the pickling liquid and keeping them crisp. The vegetables occasionally include a red chili for a spicy note and color contrast. They are exceedingly simple to make and I often serve them to dinner guests to set a mood. If you slice the vegetables so that they are very thin, you can macerate them in a sugar and rice vinegar pickling liquid for about 1 hour, serving them as "instant pickles." If the vegetables are cut thick, you can put them in a jar filled with the same pickling liquid and refrigerate them for at least 3 days. These starters are terrific served with any grilled meat or seafood.

2 to 3 large carrots, peeled and julienned

1 small daikon, peeled, halved lengthwise, and julienned

1 English (hothouse) cucumber, peeled, halved lengthwise, seeded, and cut into ¼-inch-by-2-inch-long slices

2 tablespoons kosher salt

6 tablespoons sugar

1 cup rice vinegar

1 or 2 red Thai chilies, stemmed, halved lengthwise, and seeded (optional)

1. In a large bowl, toss the carrots, daikon, and cucumber with the salt. Let stand for 1 hour. Drain, squeezing the vegetables to get rid of their excess water. Put the vegetables in a resealable plastic bag.

2. In a small bowl, whisk together the sugar and rice vinegar until the sugar is completely dissolved. Add to the vegetables, along with the chili(es) (if using). Seal the bag, squeezing any air out. Let stand for at least 1 hour. The longer the vegetables marinate, the more pickled they will taste. Eat as an accompaniment to any grilled protein. It cuts the fat and introduces a nice crunchy texture to the tender meat.

NOTES: The thinner the cut of the vegetable, the softer it will become while pickling. For instant, 1-hour pickles, cut the vegetables thin so that they will absorb flavor but still have some crunch (they will be slightly wilted). If you want to make the pickles ahead of time, cut them thick (¼ inch or more) and pickle them for at least 3 days or up to 1 week, refrigerated.

The longer the vegetables sit in the pickling liquid, the softer the texture and the more pronounced the flavor.

ASIAN COLESLAW

Serves 6 to 8

This Asian version of coleslaw starts with shredded savoy cabbage, carrots, and thinly sliced red onion and then becomes something entirely new. The traditional Western mayonnaise, sugar, and vinegar dressing is replaced by a fish sauce, palm sugar, and lime juice version, turning a basic recipe into an exciting and some-what exotic side dish. Thai basil adds a licorice-like note at the finish, but you can also use delicate cilantro leaves for a different, yet just as refreshing version. Serve with any grilled meat or seafood recipe.

⅓ cup fish sauce

⅓ cup fresh lime juice

⅓ cup palm sugar or granulated sugar

1 tablespoon vegetable oil

1 large garlic clove, minced

2 red Thai chilies, stemmed, seeded, and minced

1 small savoy or green cabbage, cored and finely shredded

3 large carrots, peeled and finely julienned

1 small to medium red onion, finely sliced

12 large fresh Thai basil leaves or 1 cup fresh cilantro leaves

In a large salad bowl, whisk together the fish sauce, lime juice, and sugar until the sugar is completely dissolved. Whisk in the oil until smooth. Add the garlic and chilies. Add the cabbage, carrots, and red onion and toss until evenly coated. Cover and refrigerate for 30 minutes to 1 hour to allow the flavors to blend. Drain and transfer to a serving dish. Serve at room temperature, gar-nished with the basil or cilantro.

NOTE: The leaves of a green cabbage are firmer than those of a savoy cabbage. If you plan to make the coleslaw more than 1 hour ahead of time, use green cab-bage. It will retain its crunchy texture better.

FRESH ZUCCHINI SALAD

Serves 6 to 8

This delicate and refreshing salad is perfect as an accompaniment to any miso- or soy sauce–marinated meat. The zucchini is raw and sliced paper-thin, making for a vegetable side dish that is both crunchy and tender in the same bite. The zucchini will give up some of its natural juices while curing. Those who like a bit of a hot note can sprinkle a small amount of red pepper flakes on the salad for both color and flavor contrast. Serve with Sweet Miso–Marinated Fish (page 115) and Green Tea and Plum Soba Medley (page 69).

¼   cup mirin (sweet sake)

¼   cup thin soy sauce

1   tablespoon rice vinegar

1   teaspoon dark sesame oil

Freshly ground black pepper to taste

4   small to medium firm zucchini, sliced into paper-thin rounds

2   scallions, trimmed and cut into thin diagonal slices (white and green parts)

Red pepper flakes to taste (optional)

In a salad bowl, whisk together the mirin, soy sauce, rice vinegar, sesame oil, and black pepper. Toss the zucchini and half of the scallions with the dressing and let stand for 30 minutes. Drain. Transfer to a serving bowl, and garnish with the remaining scallions and red pepper flakes, if using.

SWEET SUMMER CORN AND EDAMAME SALAD WITH WALNUT-MISO DRESSING

Serves 6 to 8

Tangy rice vinegar and sweet and salty miso are wonderful counterpoints to the smoky, nutty character of the toasted walnuts in the salad. Minced red onion lends a pungent note on the finish. While edamame are perfect for this dish and are usually available in the frozen foods section of your market, you can also use equal parts coarsely chopped yellow and green beans as an alternative.

2   ears yellow corn, grilled or steamed

¼   cup shiro-miso (white miso)

¼   cup mirin (sweet sake)

¼   cup rice vinegar

1½ to 2 tablespoons finely grated fresh ginger or ginger juice (see page 22)

⅓   cup walnut halves, toasted and ground (see note), plus 4 to 6 walnut halves, toasted and crushed (optional)

2   tablespoons vegetable oil

     Three 14-ounce bags frozen edamame, steamed and shelled (about 3 cups)

¼   small red onion, minced

Using a large, sharp knife, cut the kernels from the ears of corn. You should have about 1 cup of kernels. In a large salad bowl, whisk together the shiro-miso, mirin, rice vinegar, and ginger until smooth. Add the ground walnuts and oil and stir until well combined. Add the edamame and corn kernels and toss. Transfer to a serving dish and garnish with the crushed walnuts (if using) and the red onion.

NOTE: To toast walnuts, follow the instructions for toasting sesame seeds (see page 25). To grind the toasted walnuts, put the walnut halves in a mini food processor and pulse until fine. Put the ground nuts in a fine-mesh sieve over a bowl and shake the sieve as you would to sift flour. Any walnut pieces left behind in the sieve should be processed in the food processor again. Repeat as many times as necessary to achieve a powder consistency.

ASIAN PEAR SALAD

Serves 6 to 8

One of my favorite salads is Korean julienned Asian pear and raw beef, and I offer it here with julienned Garlic–Pepper Marinated Hanger Steak. For an interesting and mildly spicy version, add a small amount of Sweet and Sour Chili and Bean Paste to the dressing. The salad is so flavorful that the meat can also be eliminated completely.

1 teaspoon dark sesame oil

2 teaspoons rice vinegar

½ teaspoon Sweet and Sour Chili and Bean Paste (page 49; optional)

2 Asian pears, peeled, cored, and julienned (see note, page 91)

1 cup julienned Garlic-Pepper Marinated Hanger Steak (page 136; optional)

In a bowl, whisk together the sesame oil, rice vinegar, and chili paste, if using. With two forks (or your fingers), gently toss the pears with the dressing. Garnish the pear salad with the grilled meat, if you like.

SOUR MANGO SALAD

Serves 6 to 8

This is my interpretation of the popular Southeast Asian green papaya salad. Green papayas are readily available in Asian markets, but—unlike mangos—are probably not to be found at your local supermarket. Using underripe mangos yields a salad with sour and subtle sweet notes. The sweet lime and fish sauce dressing causes the julienned mango to soften just enough to become tender, while still retaining most of its crispness. And to complete this culinary balancing act, the unripe mango's natural sour flavor becomes mildly sweet with the sugar. Serve with Lemongrass and Kaffir Lime Leaf Marinated Pork Skewers (page 132) and jasmine rice.

⅓ cup fresh lime or lemon juice

¼ cup fish sauce

¼ cup sugar

3 large unripe mangos, peeled, halved lengthwise, pitted, and julienned

3 carrots, peeled and julienned

2 or 3 red Thai chilies, stemmed, seeded, and sliced into thin rounds

⅓ cup unsalted roasted peanuts, finely crushed

⅓ cup packed fresh Thai basil or cilantro leaves

In a medium bowl, whisk together the lime or lemon juice, fish sauce, and sugar until the sugar is completely dissolved. Put the mangos, carrots, and chilies in a resealable plastic bag. Add the dressing and seal the bag, squeezing any air out. Holding on to the ends, shake the bag to distribute the dressing throughout. Let stand for 20 minutes. Drain and transfer to a serving bowl or plate and garnish with the crushed peanuts and Thai basil or cilantro leaves. Serve at room temperature or lightly chilled.

NOTE: Not all ingredients are created equal, so adjust the seasoning as you go. Taste the dressing prior to adding to the ingredients to make sure the sour, salty, and sweet notes are balanced. Adjust the seasoning according to the acidity and sugar levels of the mangos and the salt content of the fish sauce.

SPICY CUCUMBER AND RED ONION SALAD

Serves 6 to 8

This classic lightly pickled Thai side dish is eaten with all sorts of foods, ranging from satays (page 123) to curries. Sweet, sour, and spicy on the finish, it is wonderfully simple to make. The flavor secret here is the intermingling of spicy Thai chilies, slightly bitter onion, salt–cured cucumbers, and sweetened rice vinegar pickling liquid.

2 English (hothouse) cucumbers, peeled, halved lengthwise, seeded and cut into ¼-inch-thick diagonal slices

2 teaspoons kosher salt

1 cup rice vinegar

⅓ cup sugar

1 red onion, sliced into thin wedges

1 or 2 red Thai chilies, stemmed, halved lengthwise, seeded, and thinly sliced crosswise

1. In a large sieve set over a bowl, toss the cucumbers with the salt and drain for 1 hour.

2. Meanwhile, in another bowl, whisk together the rice vinegar and sugar until the sugar is completely dissolved. Transfer this liquid to a resealable gallon plastic bag and add the drained cucumbers, onion, and chilies. Squeezing out the air, seal the bag. Holding on to the ends, shake to coat the pieces evenly. Let stand at room temperature for 1 hour before serving or refrigerate for up to 1 week.

BRAISED COLORFUL BELL PEPPER SALAD

Serves 6 to 8

2 green bell peppers

2 orange bell peppers

2 red bell peppers

2 yellow bell peppers

2 tablespoons vegetable oil

6 garlic cloves, minced

Grated zest and juice of 1½ lemons

Kosher salt and freshly ground black pepper to taste

Many markets now carry bell peppers in yellow, orange, and purple as well as the familiar red and green ones, and this evolution inspired me to create this sweet and tangy braised bell pepper salad. It is deep in flavor, and each pepper retains its vivid color. (A guest once commented that the colors were reminiscent of spring, summer, and autumn.) I do not use purple peppers here simply because they are green on the inside, but if you have some do not hesitate to add them. Each pepper is first charred on the grill. This adds a smoky aroma to the dish and allows you to ease the skins off, too. Much like the Smoky Eggplant Caviar (page 95), this bell pepper salad is rich and best eaten in small portions. I generally serve both in the same meal because they complement each other well, offering a variety of textures, colors, and flavors. This salad is even more delicious the next day.

1. Prepare a hot fire in a charcoal grill, or preheat a gas grill to 500°F (high). Grill the peppers, turning them frequently, until charred on all sides, about 5 minutes. Place the peppers in a paper bag or wrap them in aluminum foil. Let cool for 30 minutes, scrape the skin off, halve the peppers, and remove the seeds and stems. Cut the peppers lengthwise into ½-inch-thick strips and set aside.

2. In a saucepan, heat the oil over medium-high heat. Stir-fry the garlic until golden and fragrant, about 5 minutes. Add the peppers and reduce the heat to medium-low. Add the lemon juice, salt, and pepper and partially cover. Simmer, stirring occasionally, until tender, about 45 minutes. The juices should have evaporated by at least half, leaving just enough to keep the dish moist; otherwise, simmer another 15 minutes. Remove from the heat and stir in the zest. Serve at room temperature or lightly chilled.

SUNCHOKES BRAISED IN SAKE

Serves 6 to 8

Reminiscent of artichoke hearts in flavor, sunchokes, also known as Jerusalem artichokes, are tubers that grow in clusters. Here, they are braised in sake or beer. (I prefer the sake because it gives the dish a subtle and interesting fermented–rice background note.) Sweetened with caramelized onions and garlic, the dish complements grilled meats perfectly. Because they are heartier than most summer vegetables, sunchokes are especially welcome from late summer to early fall, with meals more attuned to cooler temperatures.

2   tablespoons vegetable oil

2   large garlic cloves, minced

1   large Vidalia or yellow onion, finely chopped

1½ pounds sunchokes, charred, (see page 87), peeled, and diced

1   cup sake or Asian blond beer

¼   cup packed fresh cilantro leaves, minced

    Kosher salt and freshly ground black pepper to taste

In a medium saucepan, heat the oil over medium heat. Add the garlic and stir-fry until fragrant, about 1 minute. Add the onion and stir-fry until golden, about 10 minutes. Add the sunchokes, sake, and cilantro. Season with salt and pepper. Reduce the heat to medium-low, partially cover, and simmer until the sunchokes are tender and the liquid has evaporated, about 35 minutes.

KABOCHA PUMPKIN WITH SWEET AND SAVORY MUSHROOM SAUCE

Serves 6 to 8

Japanese kabocha pumpkins are small, with dark green skins and deep-orange flesh. I first had them in Kyoto as part of an elaborate kaiseki meal and was delighted with them. Similar in texture and sweetness to a cross between sweet potato and butternut squash, kabocha can be steamed and drizzled with a kelp-infused soy and mirin sauce. I have added julienned fresh shiitake mushrooms to the sauce for a tender, contrasting texture and a more pronounced earthy flavor. The kelp stock used for making the sauce is a Japanese classic that is used in soups, stir-fries, or stews. It adds a "flavor of the sea" note to foods and allows for the blending of pungent ingredients such as those used here. For best results, make the kelp stock the night before. If time is of the essence, however, see the variation.

One 2-by-4-inch piece *kombu* (kelp) strip

2 cups plus 2 tablespoons spring or filtered water

1 small kabocha pumpkin, peeled, seeded, and cut into 1-inch-thick wedges

½ cup mirin (sweet sake)

¼ cup thin soy sauce

1 teaspoon dark sesame oil

1 tablespoon tapioca starch, potato starch, or cornstarch

Freshly ground black pepper to taste

6 fresh shiitake mushrooms, stemmed and julienned

Toasted sesame seeds for garnish (see page 25)

1. Wipe the kelp with a damp cloth and place in a bowl with the 2 cups water. Steep at least 12 hours or overnight at room temperature.

2. In a covered steamer over simmering water, steam the pumpkin until tender, 10 to 15 minutes. Transfer to a deep serving plate or bowl. Meanwhile, in a saucepan, combine the kombu stock, mirin, soy sauce, and sesame oil. Bring to a boil over high heat and reduce the heat to low. Stir together the starch and 2 tablespoons water until smooth. Add to the saucepan along with the mushrooms. Cook, stirring until thickened, about 3 minutes. Season with black pepper to taste, pour over the pumpkin, sprinkle lightly with toasted sesame seeds, and serve.

Variation

If you are pressed for time and cannot make the kombu stock the night before, here is a quick solution: In a saucepan, combine the kombu, 2 cups water, mirin, soy sauce, and sesame oil and bring to a boil over high heat. Reduce the heat to low and simmer for 30 minutes. Stir together the starch and 2 tablespoons water and add to the saucepan along with the mushrooms. Cook until thickened, about 3 minutes. Pour the thickened broth with mushrooms over the pumpkin and serve, sprinkled lightly with toasted sesame seeds.

GRILLED TOFU WITH GINGER-SOY DRESSING

Serves 6 to 8

Firm tofu, when grilled, is transformed into something completely new. Grilling makes the tofu cakes wonderfully crisp on the outside and tender on the inside. Drizzled with a combination of soy sauce, sesame oil, ginger, and scallions, this dish offers nutty, salty, spicy, and refreshing palate-cleansing notes all throughout the meal. Served with a side of baby greens tossed in Miso Salad Dressing (page 39) and Sushi Rice in Fried Tofu Pockets (page 64), the dish makes for an easy-to-prepare light but nourishing summer meal, and is a wonderful vegetarian main dish. Or, serve it as a side dish with Spicy Sweet Soy Sauce Marinated Chicken (page 121) for a heartier meal.

3   pounds firm tofu, each cake cut into six ¾-inch-thick crosswise rectangular slices

¼   cup thin soy sauce

2   tablespoons vegetable oil, plus more for brushing

2   teaspoons dark sesame oil

1 to 1½ tablespoons finely grated fresh ginger

2   scallions, trimmed and cut into paper-thin diagonal slices (white and green parts)

    Red pepper flakes for garnish

    Toasted sesame seeds for garnish (see page 25)

1. Line a plate with a double layer of paper towels, then place the tofu slices in a single layer on top. Place another double layer of paper towels on top and refrigerate for 2 hours.

2. In a small bowl, whisk together the soy sauce, 2 tablespoons vegetable oil, and the sesame oil. Add the ginger and scallions and stir. Set aside.

3. Brush each tofu slice with vegetable oil on both sides.

4. Prepare a hot fire in a charcoal grill, or preheat a gas grill to 500°F (high). Grill the tofu slices, turning them once, until heated through and golden, about 2 minutes per side. Place the tofu slices on a serving plate. Spoon the dressing over and around each piece of tofu. Sprinkle lightly with red pepper flakes and toasted sesame seeds and serve.

GRILLED FRUIT

Serves 6 to 8

1   mango, peeled, pitted, and cut into ½-inch-thick slices

1   pineapple, peeled, cored, and cut into ½-inch-thick rounds

1   firm papaya, peeled, seeded, and cut into ½-inch-thick rounds

2   plantains, peeled and cut into ½-inch-thick diagonal slices (see note)

2   bananas, peeled and halved lengthwise or 6 Asian bananas, peeled (see note)

2   Asian pears, peeled (optional), cored, and cut into ½-inch-thick rounds (see note)

2   Granny Smith apples, peeled (optional), cored, and cut into ½-inch-thick rounds

2   peaches or nectarines, peeled (optional), halved, and pitted

4   red, green, or purple plums, halved and pitted

3   Fuyu persimmons, peeled, halved, seeds removed (if any)

4   citrus fruit, such as lemons and oranges, scrubbed and cut into ¼-inch-thick rounds

    Vegetable oil for brushing

    Kosher salt and freshly ground black pepper to taste (optional)

Fruit can be grilled as simply as vegetables and afford you and your guests a range of new flavor experiences with little extra effort. Sprinkling them with some salt will deepen the sweetness of the fruit. Cooking is a great remedy for underripe and somewhat flavorless fruit; it brings out the wonderful floral aromas of certain Asian fruits, such as mangos, Asian bananas, Asian pears, Fuyu persimmons, and others.

1. Lightly brush each fruit piece with oil. Season with salt and pepper to taste (if desired) prior to grilling or just as the fruit comes off the grill.

2. Prepare a medium-hot fire in a charcoal grill, or preheat a gas grill to 400°F (medium-high). Place the fruit directly on the grill grate or use a grill basket. Grill until lightly browned, about 5 minutes.

NOTES: Available green to yellow, plantains are about twice the size of regular bananas. Unripe green types are always cooked, while the sweeter ripe yellow ones can be eaten cooked or raw. Unlike regular bananas, cooked plaintains retain their shape. Use either green or yellow in this recipe. Available mostly in Latino markets.

While several varieties of Asian bananas exist, generally the fruit is about one-third the size of regular bananas. The skin is a golden yellow, and the fruit has a pinkish golden flesh. It has a distinct floral note. Available mostly in Asian or Latino markets.

Several varieties of Asian pears exist, all with a very thin bronze-colored skin and a juicy, crisp flesh. This globe-shaped pear is mild in flavor and retains its texture rather well, never turning mealy. Asian pears can be found in Asian and occasionally Western markets.

GRILLED VEGETABLES

Serves 6 to 8

½ cup vegetable oil

2 tablespoons dark sesame oil

1 bunch asparagus

2 small to medium zucchini, sliced lengthwise into ¼-inch-thick pieces

2 small to medium yellow squash, sliced lengthwise into ¼-inch-thick pieces

12 medium to large fresh shiitake mushrooms, stemmed

4 heads bok choy

2 small to medium Japanese eggplants, cut into ¼-inch-thick diagonal slices

4 ears corn, silks and all but last layer of husks removed

1 each yellow, red, green, and orange bell pepper, quartered lengthwise, stemmed, and seeded

1 large sweet potato, scrubbed and cut into ¼-inch-thick diagonal slices

1 small to medium taro root, peeled and cut into ¼-inch-thick rounds

Kosher salt and freshly ground black pepper to taste

Miso Salad Dressing for serving (page 39)

This is a vegetable medley where, in essence, anything goes. Familiar foods such as zucchini, yellow squash, bell pepper, eggplant, white potato, sweet potato, asparagus, mushroom, and tomato (technically a fruit) will all work perfectly. I have also added a few Asian foods for those who would like to try something a bit different: bok choy, Japanese eggplant, shiitake mushrooms, and taro root. Personal preferences count for a lot here, as does seasonal availability. One of the great joys of grilling vegetables is that you can take advantage of market specials. Note that testing for doneness is a bit of an art. In general, firm foods like potatoes or taro root need to become soft and tender; soft foods like tomatoes need to get warm without falling apart. Thin foods like asparagus need to be paid attention to and turned frequently. Do not hesitate to add fruits such as apple and pear to the mix. This recipe includes starchy vegetables and makes an excellent vegetarian meal.

1. In a bowl, combine the vegetable and sesame oils. Lightly brush each vegetable piece with the mixed oils. Sprinkle lightly with salt and pepper.

2. Prepare a medium-hot fire in a charcoal grill, or preheat a gas grill to 400°F (medium-high). Place the vegetables directly on the grill grate or use grill baskets. Grill the asparagus, zucchini, yellow squash, and shiitakes until tender but slightly firm, 1 to 2 minutes per side, flipping frequently. Grill the bok choy a couple of minutes total. Grill the eggplant 2 to 3 minutes on each side. Grill the corn until golden, about 10 minutes, turning frequently. Grill the bell peppers, sweet potato, and taro root until tender, 5 to 10 minutes, turning occasionally.

3. Serve hot from the grill, with the dipping sauce on the side.

NOTE: It is important to "doctor" your vegetables when grilling them at a medium-high temperature. Turning them frequently will prevent burning. This temperature will crisp the vegetables, without making them soggy.

GRILLED BABY EGGPLANTS WITH SWEET GINGER-MISO PASTE

Serves 6 to 8

This is one of the most delicious ways to serve eggplant that I know. Halved, scored on the skin side, and served with a thick miso sauce spread on the meaty side, it is earthy, sweet, nutty in flavor, and incredibly tender. Grilling the egg-plant adds a smoky flavor to the tender flesh. A light dish, it will become a favorite quickly. The ginger–miso paste is made with mirin, grated ginger, sesame oil, and shiro–miso. If you like, double the ginger–miso paste and serve some on the side as a dip.

3   tablespoons sugar

3   tablespoons sake

2   tablespoons mirin (sweet sake)

1   tablespoon rice vinegar

⅓   cup shiro-miso (white miso)

1   tablespoon finely grated fresh ginger

¼   cup vegetable oil

1   teaspoon dark sesame oil

6   baby purple eggplants (about 4 inches long), halved length-wise through the stem

Toasted sesame seeds for garnish (see page 25)

1. In a bowl, whisk together the sugar, sake, mirin, and rice vinegar until the sugar is completely dissolved. Add the shiro-miso and ginger and whisk until well combined. Set aside.

2. In another bowl, combine the vegetable and sesame oils. Score the eggplant halves on the skin side in a crisscross pattern every ½ inch or so. Brush each piece with the oil mixture.

3. Prepare a medium-hot fire in a charcoal grill, or preheat a charcoal grill to 400°F (medium-high). Grill the eggplant, skin side down, until the skin and meat are soft, 3 to 5 minutes. Flip and grill the second side until golden and very tender, 3 to 5 minutes more.

4. Place the eggplant halves, flesh side up, on a platter. Spread each half with about 1 tablespoon of the ginger-miso paste. Sprinkle lightly with toasted sesame seeds and serve.

SMOKY EGGPLANT CAVIAR

Serves 6 to 8

Fragrant with sweet onions, cilantro, and ginger, this eggplant caviar makes for a wonderful dip or spread. A very light bitterness comes from braising the eggplant in blond beer. (If you do not like beer, you can use rice wine, such as Japanese sake, instead—the flavor will be different but equally delicious.) A simple vegetarian dish, this dip is amazingly complex in flavor. The secret is creating the dish layer by layer. First, the eggplant is charred, and the blackened skin is then peeled and discarded, leaving behind a delicious, smoky meat. Vidalia onions, which are especially sweet, add another flavor note. Caramelizing them enhances their sweetness, counterbalancing the smoky eggplant. The two are then braised with either beer or sake. The garlic and ginger add a mild spicy character, while fresh cilantro leaves refresh the palate. Serve with Parathas (page 62) or Scallion Flat Breads (page 59) for dipping, or use the caviar as a spread for any wrap sandwich.

3   large globe purple eggplants

⅓ to ½ cup vegetable oil

2   large garlic cloves, minced

1 to 1½ tablespoons finely grated fresh ginger

1   large Vidalia or yellow onion, finely chopped

1   cup Asian blond beer or sake

½   cup packed fresh cilantro leaves, minced

Kosher salt and freshly ground black pepper to taste

Paprika for dusting

1. Prepare a hot fire in a charcoal grill, or preheat a gas grill to 500°F (high). Grill the eggplants, turning them frequently, until charred on all sides, 5 to 10 minutes total. Place the eggplants in a paper bag or wrap them in aluminum foil. Let cool for 30 minutes. Scrape the skin off. Coarsely chop the eggplant into ½-inch pieces and set aside.

2. In a skillet, heat the oil over medium-high heat. Add the garlic and ginger and stir-fry until fragrant and lightly golden, about 5 minutes. Add the onion and stir-fry until deep golden, 10 to 15 minutes. Add the eggplant and stir to distribute the ingredients evenly. Add the beer or sake, cover, and reduce the heat to low. Simmer the eggplant, stirring occasionally, until very soft and all of the liquids have evaporated, 30 to 45 minutes. Stir in the cilantro, season with salt and pepper, and transfer the eggplant caviar to a serving dish. Garnish with a light dusting of paprika. Serve at room temperature.

NOTE: Braised dishes are always best the second day. This eggplant dish is no different. If you have the time, make it the day before and refrigerate it overnight, allowing the flavors to blend. The next day, bring the dish to room temperature prior to serving.

CHAPTER **6** | # FISH AND SHELLFISH

Those of you whose idea of grilled fish starts with tuna and ends with salmon have a pleasant surprise in store. Tuna and salmon are great, of course, and I cover them here, but an extraordinary variety of grilled fish is as easy to find in Asia as hot dogs in New York or pretzels in Philadelphia, and all sorts of recipes evolve from this expansive culinary tradition. On a very modest level, consider the sidewalk vendors who offer small fish such as pomfret or butterfish grilled whole. Generally, these sweet little morsels are unseasoned, cooked until crisp, and eaten—sometimes bones and all—with a dipping sauce. The vendors oil and grill the fish until they are just crisp enough to peel off the grate, and then flip them for the finish. The whole affair takes less than 10 minutes. Offered with a bowl of steamed rice and a side of pickled vegetables, it makes for a popular light, balanced, healthful, and inexpensive lunch.

From this very simple grilled fish recipe (my version uses sardines), myriad possibilities unfold. The key is variety, and here, as elsewhere in this book, I have borrowed from dozens of classic recipes, distilling some of the best examples and combining flavors from all over Asia to create earthy, spicy, sweet, savory, and tangy combinations. All sorts of fish can be spiced, herbed, marinated, wrapped, chopped and made into patties, and—in a variation— steamed over an open fire (the pot goes on the grill). I should note here that Asians absolutely depend on freshness in fish as a starting point. Fresh fish is the most flavorful, the healthiest, the firmest, and generally the best for grilling (and eating).

The freshness of fish is easiest to judge when the fish is whole: the skin should be shiny; the body should be plump, fleshy, and firm; the eyes should be bright and round, never sunken or dull. Remember that fish is mostly water, and that its moisture content should be high. Determining freshness in fillets or steaks is more difficult, but there are a few things to look for. Fillets should be moist and firm, especially around the edges, and should never be dried out or cracked. Look for bright-colored flesh from the center to the edge. If the color is even partially dull, do not purchase the fish. A word of caution, some fishmongers do not get deliveries on Sundays or Mondays, so if a fish looks less than fresh, never hesitate to ask about its day of arrival.

Many fish are cooked and served whole in Asia, symbolizing prosperity and reflecting a Buddhist (and at this point, pan-Asian) tradition that values anything served whole. It also embodies a peasant notion that tries to make use of all parts of any animal. This not only makes for a dramatic presentation, it ensures that the sweetest meat—which is always in the head—makes it to the table. Technically, you can grill any fish and many shellfish whole. Grilling outdoors is the preferred way to go here. The technique allows the excess oils to drip through and out of the fish, making it rich but delicate in flavor.

Fish fillets, too, can be grilled, the secret being to stay away from overly thin fish such as flounder and sole. Marinades are particularly well suited to firm fish fillets such as cod, haddock, bass, sea bass, salmon, red snapper, or mackerel.

Larger fish such as tuna and salmon make wonderful steaks, and I give a recipe for both salmon fillet and steak with a tuna steak variation. Because these are fallbacks for guests who do not eat meat or who are dieting, they can seem a bit predictable. You can spark them up with my sweet, dark, and citrus-noted Lemon-and-Ginger-Infused Soy Sauce (page 40)—my version of Japanese ponzu—applying it before cooking, then again when the dish is served. You can also brush oil on a plain salmon or tuna steak and serve it with Ginger and Scallion Salt Dip (page 45) over rice for an even simpler, yet just as tasty dish.

The key to grilling any thick-cut fish steak is having the fire hot enough to sear it on the outside while just cooking it through on the inside. Some Asian (and French) chefs tend to serve their fish translucent, almost raw, on the inside, especially if it is very fresh. They believe that the texture and flavor are best this way, and that the fish retains more of its natural nutrients and vitamins. Many Americans tend to shy away from this "almost raw at the center" technique, however, so make sure you gauge your guests' preferences with fish steaks the way you would with beefsteaks. Salmon and tuna are delicious cooked medium to medium-rare. Thinner steaks require quick flipping on the grill so as not to become overcooked. I prefer 1-inch-thick tuna and salmon steaks.

They are more forgiving on the grill, especially when you want to crisp the outside while keeping the inside tender and translucent.

Many types of shellfish also grill beautifully. They can be eaten right off the grill with simple starch and salad accompaniments, of course, but they also offer other opportunities. My Vietnamese-inspired shrimp sausages with Vietnamese "table salad" are a case in point. This version shapes the fresh shrimp paste into slender shrimp sausages, which are sliced on the diagonal and presented on a bed of tossed rice vermicelli with julienned carrots, cucumber, shredded lettuce, and mint leaves.

Fish patties may seem like an odd item for a grill book, but I assure you they work as well as hamburgers. The patties served in Thai and Indonesians restaurants are often white fish mixed with a spice paste and served with a sweet and tangy, sometimes spicy, sauce. Even the most skeptical "anti-fish-patty" guest will be delightfully surprised with these. Crisp on the outside, moist on the inside, they never have an unpleasant or dominant fishy taste. My version of Thai and Indonesian fish patties incorporates a yellow spice paste, distributing the flavors throughout the fish, which has first been processed to a fine consistency. When the patties hit the grill, you can smell the lemongrass, galangal, kaffir lime leaves, garlic, and shallots. Served with a sweet Thai basil and fresh lemon dressing, crispy and fragrant Fish Patties (page 113) are perfect with steamed Herbal Sticky Rice in Bamboo Leaves (page 67) and Spicy Cucumber and Red Onion Salad (page 85) on the side.

Last but not least, I have developed two hybrid Asian-flavored clambakes. While one is and one is not technically a grilled dish, both are similar in spirit. The first has the seafood and other ingredients cooked directly on a grill over a pit fire; the second employs a large pot set over a fire, affording an opportunity to create a broth in the process. The broth tastes of the sea, with various kinds of seafood sweetening the mix.

GINGER-AND-SCALLION-INFUSED SCALLOPS WITH BLACK BEAN SAUCE

Serves 6 to 8

Two Asian recipes are better than one here. In Cantonese restaurants, you will often find menu items such as stir-fried lobster with ginger and scallions, and steamed shrimp–stuffed tofu with black bean sauce. I like the taste of both sauces at the same time. The thick, juicy scallops are delicious over rice, especially when topped with Chinese Black Bean Sauce. Braised Colorful Bell Pepper Salad (page 87) is a beautiful vegetable accompaniment.

1 to 1½ tablespoons finely grated fresh ginger

3 scallions, trimmed and minced (white and green parts)

2 tablespoons Shaoxing rice wine or sake

1 tablespoon vegetable oil, plus more for grilling

36 large sea scallops

12 long bamboo skewers

Kosher salt and freshly ground black pepper to taste

Steamed rice for serving (page 68)

Chinese Black Bean Sauce (page 44) for drizzling

1. In a bowl, mix together the ginger, scallions, rice wine, and oil. Put the scallops in a resealable gallon plastic bag. Add the marinade and, squeezing the air out, seal the bag. Holding on to the ends, shake the bag to coat the pieces evenly with the marinade. Refrigerate for 4 hours, turning the bag over every 30 minutes or so to redistribute the marinade.

2. Soak the bamboo skewers in water for 30 minutes. Meanwhile prepare a hot fire in a charcoal grill, or preheat a gas grill to 500°F (high). Thread 6 scallops, through the sides, on 2 parallel skewers. Place the skewered scallops in a single layer on a platter and lightly salt and pepper each side. Grill the scallops until golden, about 2 minutes on each side. Serve the scallops over rice, drizzled with 1 to 2 tablespoons of black bean sauce.

SPICY THAI BASIL AND LIME MARINATED JUMBO SHRIMP

Serves 6 to 8

24 jumbo tiger shrimp (about 10 per pound)

¼ cup fish sauce

¼ cup fresh lime or lemon juice

¼ cup palm sugar or granulated sugar

1 tablespoon vegetable oil

1 large garlic clove, finely grated

¼ cup packed fresh Thai basil, mint, or cilantro leaves, minced

1 or 2 red Thai chilies, stemmed, seeded, and minced

Jumbo black (sometimes called "blue") tiger shrimp are meaty, sweet, and firm and perfect for grilling. Generally, I buy them "Asian style," meaning whole, with the heads still on, because the heads are full of sweet tomalley and roe. (Guests can eat or dispense with the heads as they please, but the whole shrimp make for a nice presentation.) The marinade combines Thai basil and lime with a base of fish sauce and sugar. Tiger shrimp are particularly good with this marinade, their sweet flavor and firm texture holding up to the bold flavors. You can slice and toss the shrimp and vegetables in a big bowl and serve the ingredients like a salad, too. The marinade in all its forms is well suited for other seafood, including scallops, lobster tails, squid, and fish steaks.

1. Using a paring knife, cut through the back shell of each shrimp. Remove the dark vein. Run your forefinger between the shell and the flesh of each shrimp, separating but not removing the shell from the flesh.

2. In a large bowl, whisk together the fish sauce, lime or lemon juice, and sugar until the sugar is completely dissolved. Add the oil, garlic, basil, and chili. If you wish, pour the marinade in a blender and pulse until smooth.

3. Place the shrimp and marinade in a resealable gallon plastic bag. Squeezing out the air, seal the bag. Holding on to the two ends, shake the bag to coat the pieces evenly with the marinade. Refrigerate for 4 hours, turning the bag over every 30 minutes or so to redistribute the marinade.

4. Prepare a hot fire in a charcoal grill, or preheat a gas grill to 500°F (high). Grill the shrimp, turning them frequently to prevent burning, until evenly pink and golden on both sides, 2 to 3 minutes.

GRILLED SHRIMP SAUSAGES

Serves 6 to 8

Firm and plump, these shrimp and toasted-rice sausages are easy to make and perfect for the grill. Based on the classic Vietnamese specialty, fresh shrimp paste molded around sugarcane and grilled, they can quickly become a family favorite. A delicate, slightly spongy texture derives from adding a small amount of baking soda to the mix. These "sausages without casing" are eaten with a sweet and sour fish sauce dressing or over a serving of Rice Vermicelli with Scallion Oil and Fresh Vegetables (page 71). Shrimp are naturally salty, so I do not season the rolls with salt. Also take into account that the shrimp sausages will be served with the fish sauce dressing, and that is well seasoned.

2 pounds headless tiger shrimp, shelled, deveined, and minced

6 tablespoons vegetable oil

2 teaspoons sugar

1 cup Toasted Rice Flour (page 54)

1½ teaspoons baking soda

4 scallions, trimmed and minced (white and green parts)

½ teaspoon freshly ground black pepper

   Sweet, Sour, and Spicy Fish Sauce Dressing (page 42) for dipping

1. In a large bowl, mix together the shrimp, 3 tablespoons of the oil, the sugar, ⅓ cup of the rice flour, the baking soda, scallions, and pepper until well combined. Cover and refrigerate for 30 minutes.

2. Put the remaining ⅔ cup toasted rice flour on a plate. Divide the shrimp mixture into 32 equal portions (about 1½ tablespoons each). Shape the portions into 2-inch-long sausages. Coat each lightly and evenly with the rice flour.

3. Prepare a medium-hot grill in a charcoal grill, or preheat a gas grill to 400°F (medium-high). Brush the shrimp sausages with the remaining 3 tablespoons of oil and grill, turning them often, until crisp, golden, and cooked through, about 3 minutes total. Serve with the dressing for dipping.

ASIAN CLAMBAKE

Serves about 12

This is my Asian-style take on an American clambake. I experienced my first clambake on a beach in the Hamptons on Long Island, New York, years ago, and never forgot it. It was enormous fun: setting out to get all the seafood, gathering the firewood and rocks, digging a fire pit, harvesting seaweed. Since then I have worked at developing a variation on the classic, using Asian aromatics such as kaffir lime leaves, lemongrass, ginger, cilantro, Thai basil, and galangal. The result is still suitable for backyard or beach, true to the original in its basic ingredients, but complex and layered with herbs. If you choose to make a fire pit, you'll want to consider using banana leaves as a lid, and you'll need to line the pit with rocks so that it keeps its shape. You can also use a stockpot over an open fire. Both make for a delicious meal.

This is an event as much as a recipe. Involve your guests and be sure to make plenty of everything, because people will want to stick around well beyond mealtime, nibbling on the leftovers. Serve this with any number of sides, including Asian Coleslaw (page 77), Herbal Sticky Rice in Bamboo Leaves (page 67), Ginger-Garlic Chili Paste (page 50), and Ginger and Scallion Salt Dip (page 45).

48 cherry clams

12 chicken legs

12 small lobsters, about 1¼ pounds each

12 large blue crabs

12 ears corn, silks and all but last layer of husk removed

12 small waxy potatoes, scrubbed

⅓ cup thinly sliced fresh ginger

⅓ cup thinly sliced fresh galangal

1 large bunch fresh Thai basil

1 large bunch fresh cilantro

24 fresh kaffir lime leaves, bruised

8 lemongrass stalks, trimmed and sliced on the diagonal (white and light green parts)

2 large Vidalia or other sweet onions, sliced into ½-inch-thick rounds

12 scallions, trimmed and lightly crushed (white and green parts)

Kosher salt and freshly crushed black pepper to taste

1. Dig a fire pit and build a fire according to the instructions on page 33. It will take about 1 hour for the fire to reduce to coals. Meanwhile, soak the clams in several changes of water to get rid of any sand.

2. Once the coals are ready, place the grill on top. Spread the clams out in an even layer and scatter the chicken legs in the center of the grill where it is the hottest. Layer with the lobsters, crabs, corn, and potatoes, scattering some ginger, galangal, Thai basil, cilantro, kaffir lime leaves, lemongrass, onions, and scallions between the layers. Sprinkle with salt and pepper.

3. Cover the pit with banana leaves and secure the leaves with rocks set on the edge. Cook for 1 hour. Remove a potato or chicken leg set closest to the edge of the grill and check for doneness.

8 ounces kelp, wiped with a damp
  cloth and soaked in water to
  cover until soft

4 large banana leaves, cleaned

NOTES: The stockpot method is a great fallback if digging a pit is too much work. In fact, not only will it be just as delicious, but you will have a broth to accompany the fruits of your labor. Use a 20-quart stockpot and fill the first 3 inches with the water used to soak the kelp. Add the kelp, chicken, clams, lobsters, crabs, corn (remove all husks), and potatoes, scattering the aromatics in between each layer. Season with salt and pepper and cover the pot with 2 layers of banana leaves. Bring to a boil. Reduce the heat to medium and cook for 30 minutes.

Additionally, you can cook Herbal Sticky Rice in Bamboo Leaves in the pot as well. Just put the packages on top of the other food.

SPICY SQUID SALAD

Serves 6 to 8

This warm salad features a beautifully balanced marinade, with tamarind, lime juice, and sugar on the tangy side, and fish sauce, garlic, onion, and Thai chili on the savory side. Good squid is tender and clean in flavor, never chewy. The sliced tomatoes, fresh Thai basil, and cilantro add another layer of texture and flavor to this appealing seafood salad.

¼ cup Tamarind Concentrate (page 55)

2 tablespoons fish sauce

1 tablespoon fresh lime juice

1 tablespoon sugar

1 large garlic clove, minced

1 small yellow onion, sliced into thin wedges

1 or 2 red Thai chilies, stemmed, seeded, and julienned

1 pound baby or medium-sized squid, skinned and cleaned, tentacles separated from body

Vegetable oil for brushing

1 ripe red tomato, seeded (see note, page 47) and cut into 8 to 10 wedges

½ cup fresh Thai basil leaves

½ cup fresh cilantro leaves

1. In a medium bowl, whisk together the tamarind concentrate, fish sauce, lime juice, and sugar until the sugar is completely dissolved. Add the garlic, onion, and chilies. Let stand for 20 minutes. Brush the squid with oil.

2. Prepare a hot fire in a charcoal grill, or preheat a gas grill to 500°F (high). Grill the squid bodies and tentacles until golden and crisp on each side, 2 to 4 minutes. Cut the bodies into ½-inch-wide rings.

3. Toss the squid with the tomato, Thai basil, cilantro, and tamarind mixture and transfer to a serving platter.

GRILLED WILD SALMON SUSHI ROLLS

Serves 6 to 8

Vegetable oil for brushing

1 pound wild Alaskan salmon
   fillets, skin on, steaks, or
   tuna steaks

1¼ cups Lemon-and-Ginger-Infused
   Soy Sauce (page 40)

2 cups short- or medium-grain
   sushi rice

4 tablespoons rice vinegar, plus
   more for forming rice

4 teaspoons sugar

¼ cup wasabi powder

2 tablespoons spring or filtered
   water

6 sheets nori

18 fresh purple or green shiso
   leaves

1 small seedless cucumber,
   julienned

1 cup clover sprouts or arugula

Wild salmon is naturally deep orange-red in color and particularly flavorful, unlike the vast majority of farm-raised salmon, which is mild in flavor and light orange. Brushed with a lemon-and-ginger-infused soy sauce, it caramelizes when grilled. Served as a sushi roll, it makes for a beautiful and delicate presentation and for a healthful meal full of varying textures and colors. The rice acts as a canvas for all the flavors to come together in a single bite. The lemon-and-ginger-infused soy sauce gives this sushi roll a deep flavoring. The shiso leaves and clover sprouts lend a slightly bitter, somewhat peppery note. Rather than use soy or tamari sauce for dipping, serve this grilled salmon maki with the pungent lemon and ginger soy sauce dip and some wasabi on the side.

Salmon fillets or steaks are also delicious grilled and topped with the lemon-and-ginger-infused soy sauce; you do not have to make sushi rolls to enjoy the fish. You can also try thick tuna steaks, seared on the outside and rare on the inside. When sliced, the tuna is also delicious drizzled with the same tangy and pungent sauce and served over a bed of baby salad greens tossed with Miso Salad Dressing (page 39).

1. Brush oil on the skin of the salmon and place the fillet skin side down on a plate. Brush some of the lemon-ginger soy sauce on the flesh side. Refrigerate for 1 hour.

2. In a medium pot, combine the rice and water to cover. Stir to level. Cover the pot and cook over medium-low heat until the rice has absorbed all of the water, about 20 minutes. Turn off the heat and fluff the rice with a spoon. Allow to rest, covered, for 10 minutes.

3. Meanwhile, in a small bowl, whisk together the 4 tablespoons rice vinegar and the sugar until the sugar is completely dissolved.

4. Transfer the cooked rice to a Japanese round wooden rice container and spread it out in a thin layer. While fanning (using a traditional bamboo paddle, a hand held paper fan, a card, or anything that works) the rice to cool it, work in the vinegar mixture. Moisten your hands with rice vinegar to keep the rice from sticking to them while dividing it into 6 equal portions. Let stand at room temperature, covered with plastic wrap.

(Cont'd)

5. Prepare an indirect fire in a charcoal grill or gas grill (page 34). Grill the salmon, skin side down, on the cooler side of the grill until the skin is golden and crisp, about 5 minutes. Meanwhile, brush some oil on the flesh side. Turn and grill on the other side for 3 minutes more. Transfer to a plate.

6. Mix the wasabi powder and 2 tablespoons water until well combined. The wasabi paste should not stick to your hands when rolled into a ball.

7. Cover a bamboo sushi mat with a layer of plastic wrap. (This will help keep the mat clean and make it easier to remove the sushi roll.) Place a sheet of nori on top of the covered mat, shiny side down. Take 1 portion of rice and spread it evenly over two-thirds of the nori sheet closest to you. Next, smear a thin layer of wasabi paste in a single line along the width of the roll. Next, overlap 3 shiso leaves on top, then some cucumber and sprouts. Finally, flake about 2 tablespoons of salmon with skin and add it across the top. Using the bamboo mat, grab hold of the thick end of the roll and roll it over the ingredients tightly. The last third of the nori sheet should be left. Roll the ingredients all the way to the end of the nori sheet. Remove each nori roll from the plastic and cut crosswise into 6 equal pieces. Serve with the lemon and ginger soy sauce dip and wasabi paste on the side.

GRILLED SARDINES

Serves 6 to 8

An acquired taste for some, a wonderful treat for others, fresh sardines are among the simplest fish to grill. Based on the grilling techniques of street vendors, this recipe is typical of the quick whole-fish meals you find all over Asia. They also have a unique flavor, and a squeeze of lime or lemon is the perfect accompaniment. When serving an Asian-inspired summer meal, I like to pair the grilled sardines with Ginger and Scallion Salt Dip (page 45), or Spicy Vinegar Dipping Sauce (page 43). The addition of rice or fresh bread and salad makes for a healthful meal.

18 sardines, cleaned, heads and tails intact

Vegetable oil for brushing

Kosher salt and freshly ground black pepper to taste

1. Brush the sardines with oil and sprinkle lightly with salt and pepper.

2. Prepare a medium-hot fire in a charcoal grill, or preheat a gas grill to 400°F (medium-high). Grill the sardines until the skin is crisp, golden, and comes off the grill without fuss, about 4 minutes per side.

FISH PATTIES

Serves 6 to 8

Fragrant with floral notes from a yellow herbal spice paste, these fish patties are popular in many Asian food cultures, and are nothing like the frozen fish sticks and patties found in American supermarkets. They are generally panfried, deep-fried, or grilled and are often served with a complementing dipping sauce. In Asia, the fish would likely be pounded by hand into a pastelike consistency. Here, to save some time, I use a food processor, which does the job just fine. To finish the patties, I dust them with toasted rice flour, which gives them a nice nutty flavor.

2   pounds cod, hake, or haddock, skin and bones removed

¾   cup Yellow Spice Paste (page 52)

1½ teaspoons baking soda

1   cup Toasted Rice Flour (page 54)

Vegetable oil for brushing

Thai Basil and Lemon Relish (page 45) for serving

1. In a food processor, process the fish to a smooth paste, about 1 minute. Add the spice paste and baking soda and continue to process until the paste is well mixed and firm and has a bit of a bounce to it, about 1 minute more.

2. Divide the paste into 32 round patties (about 1½ tablespoons each) and refrigerate for 1 hour. Dust each patty with toasted rice flour.

3. Prepare a medium-hot grill in a charcoal grill, or preheat a gas grill to 400°F (medium-high). Brush each patty with oil and grill, turning them often, until crisp, golden, and cooked through, about 3 minutes per side. Serve with the relish on the side.

SWEET MISO-MARINATED FISH

Serves 6 to 8

"Fish candy" is how I like to describe this extraordinarily delicious dish. The classic version, found in upscale Japanese restaurants, is broiled black cod cured in shiro-miso—perhaps the mildest and sweetest of the miso pastes (that is, least salty). The shiro-miso is combined with sugar and tangy sake to create a smooth, creamy marinade in which the fish is marinated for 24 to 48 hours. The longer the fish is marinated, the firmer and sweeter it becomes, hence "fish candy." While I often use black cod and other similar big, white, flaky fish, in the spring and summer I make a grilled version with mackerel. Mackerel has character and texture enough to stand up to grilling, and a sort of culinary magic happens when it is grilled. In essence, the fish offers pronounced flavors that balance perfectly against sweet notes, yielding a dish that is understated while being rich in flavor and texture. The Green Tea and Plum Soba Medley (page 69) is a perfect accompaniment.

½ cup shiro-miso (white miso)

3 tablespoons sake

3 tablespoons mirin (sweet sake)

⅓ cup sugar

4 mackerel fillets, each halved crosswise on the diagonal, or 2 pounds cod, hake, or haddock, cut into 8 equal pieces

Vegetable oil for brushing

1. In a medium bowl, whisk together the shiro-miso, sake, mirin, and sugar until the sugar is completely dissolved and the marinade is smooth.

2. Place the fish and marinade in a resealable gallon plastic bag. Squeezing out the air, seal the bag. Holding on to the ends, shake the bag to coat the pieces evenly with the marinade. Refrigerate the fish for 24 to 48 hours, turning the bag over every 2 hours or so.

3. Prepare an indirect fire in a charcoal or gas grill (see page 34). Brush each piece of fish with oil on all sides. Grill fish skin side down first, until golden crisp and cooked through, 2 to 3 minutes per side.

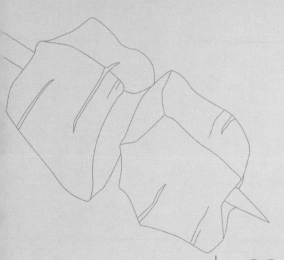

CHAPTER **7** | MEATS, POULTRY, AND GAME

Two basic philosophies exist on grilling meat: Reveal the flavor of the ingredient or transform the flavor of the ingredient. Asians have long understood this and have grilled pork and beef ribs that are heavily sauced (Country Ribs with Hoisin Sauce, page 128) as well as chicken that is barely seasoned save for a bit of ginger-and-scallion-flavored salt (page 45). The clearest example of this kind of thinking may be Texas barbecue, however. "Don't sauce" versus "sauce" is a big deal in the Lone Star State: "If you have to sauce it, it isn't done right" versus "The magic is in the sauce because it draws out the beauty of the meat."

I like my steak simple; a great cut seasoned with salt and pepper just before it hits the grill. It's mostly about revealing the quality of good meat. Some cuts are better when artfully transformed, however, especially if they are a bit tough or very strong in flavor, or when you just want a change of pace. Salt and pepper allow more of the meat, and especially its flavor-bearing fat, to come to the fore. You can add it as a dry rub, as in Kansas City or Szechwan, or a bit of vinegar, as in North Carolina or Shanghai, but it is a matter of degree and taste.

This chapter includes a range of grilled meat and poultry recipes, with a bit more emphasis on the joys of complex flavoring. Myriad herbs and spices are used on a daily basis in Asian cooking, and this is where the magic tends to lie. Generally, the Chinese and Japanese season the least, allowing the flavor of the main ingredient to come to the fore. But in many parts of Asia, long lists of herbs, spices, and condiments are used to transform a delicate piece of meat into something rather bold in flavor. For all these reasons, many of the recipes here will seem to be as much about the marinade as the meat. Fish sauce, sugar, and garlic is a common marinade used throughout Southeast Asia, including Vietnam, Cambodia, and Laos. When lemongrass, scallions, ginger, and other herbs and spices are added, the flavor notes grow deeper and more complex. The same goes for soy sauce–based marinades.

South Asian– and Indian-based ingredients broaden the range of flavors. My Punjab-inspired tandoori chicken recipe (opposite), for example, uses a yogurt-based marinade with lots of cardamom, cumin, cinnamon, cloves, and other strong flavors. The yogurt mediates the intensity of the spicing while tenderizing the meat. Tandoori marinades can also be used on lamb, fish, or sausage.

The spicy herbed marinades of Asia developed out of an ancient need to retard spoilage and preserve foodstuffs. (Inaccessible mountainous regions and very hot and humid climates often use intense spicing as a result.) These concoctions have evolved to the point where they can both transform a food and refresh the palate as you eat. They expand the enjoyment of tasting food, giving it—like a good wine—a long finish that lingers for several minutes.

The flavors of Asia can be generally described as being earthy, citrusy, and licorice-like. Kaffir lime leaves, lemongrass, Thai basil, galangal, ginger, garlic, and scallion are the basics, offering complex aromas and tastes ranging from bitter to sour, sweet, and spicy. Fish sauce or soy sauce forms a salty base that cures the herbs (causing them to release their essential oils) even as it cures the meats. Beef Filet Mignon Cubes with Sweet Lime Dipping Sauce (page 141) is a perfect example of this exquisite culinary dance.

SPICED YOGURT-MARINATED CHICKEN

Serves 6 to 8

Based on the Indian classic, tandoori chicken (originally from the Punjab), this mildly spicy dish is so fragrant it reminds me of Indian spice markets I have visited. Traditionally, red food coloring is used to lend tandoori chicken a festive red tone, a symbol of luck in many Asian cultures. The coloring offers no flavor, however, so I have opted to omit it here. Turmeric, which has a mild flavor, gives the chicken a yellow hue. Serve with Cucumber and Preserved Lemon Yogurt (page 48), Pineapple and Onion Chutney (page 46), Fresh Tomato Chutney (page 47), and Parathas (page 62).

1   **cup plain Greek yogurt**

    Grated zest and juice of 1 lemon, plus 2 lemons, each cut into 8 wedges, for garnish

2   **tablespoons coconut vinegar or rice vinegar**

1   **large shallot, finely grated**

1   **large garlic clove, finely grated**

1½ **tablespoons finely grated fresh ginger**

2   **teapoons Spice Route Blend (page 53)**

3   **pounds skinless chicken breasts and/or legs**

2   **tablespoons vegetable oil**

1. In a medium bowl, whisk together the yogurt, lemon juice, and coconut or rice vinegar until well combined. With a spoon, stir in the shallot, garlic, ginger, and lemon zest. Add the spice blend and stir until well combined. Set aside.

2. Score the chicken diagonally every 1 inch on the top side, but without hitting the bone (if you cut too close to the bone, the meat will fall off when cooked). This allows the marinade to penetrate the meat evenly and makes the chicken cook quicker. Put the chicken and marinade in a resealable gallon plastic bag. Squeezing out the air, seal the bag. Holding on to the ends, shake the bag to coat the pieces evenly with the marinade. Refrigerate for at least 12 hours, turning the bag over every hour or so.

3. Prepare a medium-hot fire in a charcoal grill, or preheat a gas grill to 400°F (medium-high). Grill the chicken, scored side down first. Turn the pieces frequently to prevent burning, and baste occasionally with vegetable oil until the juices run clear, about 15 minutes. Transfer the chicken to a serving dish and garnish with the lemon wedges.

SPICY SWEET SOY SAUCE MARINATED CHICKEN

Serves 6 to 8

½ cup thin soy sauce

1 tablespoon thick soy sauce

¼ cup Shaoxing rice wine or sake

⅓ cup sugar

1 tablespoon dark sesame oil

2 large garlic cloves, finely grated

1 scallion, trimmed and minced
   (white and green parts)

1 to 1½ tablespoons finely grated
   fresh ginger

1 red Thai chili, stemmed,
   seeded, and minced

8 whole chicken legs or whole
   breasts

My guests are often surprised at how many rich and varied flavors this easy-to-prepare chicken recipe has in each bite. Some imagine they have been served an exotic squab or game bird; others assume the preparation took hours. Amazingly rich, and as sweet and savory as it is spicy, the dish starts with a variation on a basic soy sauce marinade. In its simplest form, it combines soy sauce, garlic, and pepper. There are, however, as many variations as there are Chinese cooks. My version adds a thick soy sauce (giving the meat a nice amber tone), sesame oil for a nutty note, minced Thai chili to lift the palate, Shaoxing rice wine to round out the flavors, and grated ginger for a refreshing and light bitter finishing note. I have also tried pork with this marinade, and it is delightful. Serve with Sushi Rice in Fried Tofu Pockets (page 64) and Fresh Zucchini Salad (page 78) or mesclun greens tossed with Miso Salad Dressing (page 39).

1. In a large bowl, whisk together the thin and thick soy sauces, rice wine, and sugar until the sugar is completely dissolved. Add the sesame oil, garlic, scallion, ginger, and chili. Stir well.

2. Using a skewer, poke holes in the chicken legs or breasts. Place the chicken and marinade in a resealable gallon plastic bag. Squeezing out the air, seal the bag. Holding on to the ends, shake the bag to coat the pieces evenly with the marinade. Refrigerate for 3 to 4 hours, turning the bag over every 30 minutes or so to redistribute the marinade.

3. Prepare an indirect fire in a charcoal or gas grill (see page 34). Grill the chicken breasts or legs until crisp and cooked through, turning the meat frequently to prevent burning, 10 to 15 minutes total. Transfer chicken to a serving dish.

CHICKEN SATAY

Serves 6 to 8

1 cup unsweetened coconut milk

1 tablespoon palm sugar or granulated sugar

1 teaspoon ground coriander

½ teaspoon ground turmeric

¼ teaspoon ground cumin

2 to 3 pounds skinless, boneless chicken breasts, cut against the grain into ⅛-inch-thick slices

12 long bamboo skewers

Spicy Peanut Sauce (page 41) for dipping

Satay, originating in Southeast Asia, is skewered and grilled meat served with dipping sauces. The dish has recently gained tremendous popularity in the United States, where it has become an instant classic. It is often associated with peanut sauce in the West, but other dipping sauces are also employed. Truth be told, the marinade in this recipe is so simple and tasty that you do not need a dipping sauce. For those who love sauces, however, this satay is served with a mildly spicy coconut-based peanut sauce. For a more complex flavoring, you can replace the ground coriander, cumin, and turmeric with the same amount of Spice Route Blend (page 53), which is delicious with chicken, shrimp, and many other proteins. Satay can be chewed right off its bamboo skewer, requiring no utensils for eating and making it a great party food. Serve with Parathas (page 62) and Spicy Cucumber and Red Onion Salad (page 85).

1. In a small bowl, whisk together the coconut milk, sugar, coriander, turmeric, and cumin until well incorporated and the sugar is completely dissolved.

2. Put the chicken and marinade in a resealable gallon plastic bag. Squeezing out the air, seal the bag. Holding on to the ends, shake the bag to coat the pieces evenly with the marinade. Refrigerate for 2 hours, turning occasionally to redistribute the marinade.

3. Soak the bamboo skewers in water for 30 minutes. Meanwhile prepare a hot fire in a charcoal grill, or preheat a gas grill to 500°F (high). Thread 4 to 6 pieces of chicken on each skewer. Grill the chicken skewers, turning the pieces frequently to prevent burning, until crisp, 1 to 2 minutes per side. Serve with peanut sauce for dipping.

Variation
Substitute 24 headless jumbo tiger shrimp for the chicken. Devein each shrimp through the shell and proceed with the recipe. (Be sure to rub the marinade between the meat and the shell.)

FIVE-SPICE CHICKEN

Serves 6 to 8

This sweet and savory dry rub gives meat a delicious licorice–like flavor. In China, this is used to season chicken legs, which are then deep-fried. I like to grill the chicken legs for a lighter version of the classic. I prefer to use sweet and juicy dark meat, because its richness holds up to the pungent rub well. Serve with steamed rice, Grilled Vegetables (page 93), and mesclun tossed in Miso Salad Dressing (page 39).

1 tablespoon kosher salt

1½ teaspoons Chinese five-spice powder

1½ teaspoons sugar

½ teaspoon freshly ground black pepper

6 whole chicken legs

1. In a small bowl, mix together the salt, five-spice powder, sugar, and pepper until well combined. Set the dry rub aside.

2. Score the chicken legs every inch or so and sprinkle lightly and evenly with the dry rub. Put the chicken in a resealable gallon plastic bag. Squeezing out the air, seal the bag. Refrigerate for 2 hours.

3. Prepare an indirect fire in a charcoal or gas grill (see page 34). Grill the chicken legs until crisp and cooked through, turning the meat frequently to prevent burning, about 15 minutes. Transfer chicken to a serving dish.

NOTE: This dry rub also works well with duck breasts or lamb chops.

FIVE-SPICE MARINATED DUCK

Serves 6 to 8

⅓ cup thin soy sauce or fish sauce

⅓ cup sugar

1½ teaspoons Chinese five-spice powder

2 large garlic cloves, finely grated

1½ tablespoons finely grated fresh ginger

4 Moulard duck breast halves, or 8 Long Island duck breast halves, skin and fat removed

Magret, or Moulard duck breast, is my favorite type of red meat. It is bold in flavor, and comes with a thick layer of fat and skin. Removing this layer is good from a health perspective, but many cooks cook the breast skin-on because the fat lends flavor to the meat and the skin is delicious when crisped. I have discovered, however, that when the meat is marinated in a medley of exotic spices before cooking, the fat is not missed. The lean meat takes on a deep, complex flavor note. The trick is in the spicing. The classic Chinese five-spice powder works beautifully as a base. The addition of ginger and garlic lifts the palate. Soy sauce is used to blend the spices and herbs into a medley of spicy, sweet, salty, and bitter notes. A squeeze or two of sour lime or lemon juice may be added for a bit of refreshing tang with each bite. When served, the duck breasts are lean and complex in flavor and the spicy outer surface nicely crisped. Rack of lamb will also work with this recipe. Serve with Herbal Sticky Rice in Bamboo Leaves (page 67) and Sour Mango Salad (page 83).

1. In a large bowl, whisk together the soy sauce and sugar until the sugar is completely dissolved. Stir in the five-spice powder, garlic, and ginger until well combined.

2. Add the duck and marinade to a resealable gallon plastic bag. Squeezing out the air, seal the bag. Holding on to the ends, shake the bag to coat the pieces evenly with the marinade. Refrigerate for 6 hours, turning the bag over every 30 minutes or so to redistribute the marinade.

3. Prepare a hot fire in a charcoal grill, or preheat a gas grill to 500°F (high). Grill the duck breasts, turning them frequently to prevent burning, until crisp on the outside and medium-rare, about 6 minutes. Transfer duck to a serving dish.

BBQ PORK

Serves 6 to 8

This recipe is based on the classic Cantonese roast pork often seen hanging in the windows of Chinese restaurants in Chinatown. Sweet with honey and savory with fermented bean curd and soy sauce, the pork shoulder caramelizes when cooked, crisping the edges. The shoulder is a particularly wonderful cut for this recipe. It has just enough fat to keep the meat juicy on the inside. While using red food coloring is traditional, symbolizing luck, I have opted to omit it here as it does not add anything to the flavor. The roast pork will have a natural reddish hue because of the use of soy sauce. Serve with steamed rice, baby greens tossed in Miso Salad Dressing (page 39), and grilled corn, or serve sliced and wrapped in Scallion Flat Breads (page 59).

2	tablespoons hoisin sauce
1	cube preserved bean curd
¼	cup thin soy sauce
¼	cup sugar
1	tablespoon Shaoxing rice wine or sake
2	large garlic cloves, minced
1	teaspoon finely grated fresh ginger
2	pounds pork shoulder (pork butt), cut into long 1-inch-thick strips
¼	cup honey

1. In a bowl, whisk together the hoisin sauce, bean curd, soy sauce, sugar, rice wine, garlic, and ginger. Transfer the marinade and pork strips to a resealable gallon plastic bag. Squeezing out the air, seal the bag. Holding on to the ends, shake the bag gently to coat the strips evenly. Refrigerate and marinate for 4 to 6 hours, turning the bag every 30 minutes to redistribute the marinade.

2. Prepare a hot fire in a charcoal grill, or preheat a gas grill to 500°F (high). Grill the pork strips, turning them frequently to prevent burning, 10 to 15 minutes for medium. Remove the pork strips from the heat and immediately brush honey all over. Let rest for 15 minutes before slicing and serving.

COUNTRY RIBS WITH HOISIN SAUCE

Serves 6 to 8

⅓ cup hoisin sauce

¼ cup fish sauce

2 tablespoons sugar

2 large garlic cloves, finely grated

1½ tablespoons finely grated fresh ginger

2½ pounds boneless pork country ribs, cut into ½-inch-thick slices

Some of my Western friends are easily overwhelmed when it comes to Asian ingredients. For whatever reason—labels they can't understand, odd textures and colors, unfamiliar aromas, and so forth—they often shy away. Once they go to the market with me or watch me cook with Asian "mystery ingredients" (as one friend once described them), they are surprised at how easy it all is. A demonstration and a few explanations usually broaden their horizons. Among the mysterious and inscrutable, hoisin sauce has always been an easy item to introduce. Dark brown in color, it is mostly sweet with savory undertones much like the familiar Western barbecue sauce. After experiencing one cooking session using this soybean-based condiment, my formerly overwhelmed friends run out to buy a jar or two. Hoisin is versatile—you can slather it onto pork ribs straight from the jar, or you can make a marinade by adding fish sauce, sugar, and garlic. This recipe is a family favorite, and seems to work with everyone as a good starting point for Asian flavors. Choose meaty, juicy boneless country ribs, because they have more meat than fat and are naturally juicy and sweet. Serve with Delicate Sesame Wraps (page 61), Braised Colorful Bell Pepper Salad (page 87), and Smoky Eggplant Caviar (page 95), or with Asian Coleslaw (page 77) and Herbal Sticky Rice in Bamboo Leaves (page 67).

1. In a small bowl, whisk together the hoisin sauce, fish sauce, and sugar until the sugar is completely dissolved. Stir in the garlic and ginger and set aside.

2. Put the ribs and marinade in a resealable gallon plastic bag. Squeezing out the air, seal the bag. Holding on to the ends, shake the bag to coat the pieces evenly with the marinade. Refrigerate for 4 to 6 hours, turning the bag every 30 minutes or so to redistribute the marinade.

3. Prepare a hot fire in a charcoal grill, or preheat a gas grill to 500°F (high). Grill the ribs, turning the pieces frequently to prevent burning, until crisp and cooked through, about 6 minutes. Transfer ribs to a serving dish.

BLACK BEAN AND GARLIC MARINATED POR SHOULDER

BLACK BEAN AND GARLIC MARINATED PORK SHOULDER

Serve 6 to 8

Black bean and garlic sauce is used primarily for steamed and braised dishes, and occasionally for stir-fries, and its complex flavor goes well with pork. The flavorful pork shoulder is good cut into long thin strips, because it crisps when cooked over a hot fire. Wrapped in Delicate Sesame Wraps (page 61) with some Sweet and Sour Chili and Bean Paste (page 49) and fresh lettuce with Pickled Daikon, Carrot, and Cucumber (page 76), for example, this dish makes a wonderful lunch.

1   cup fermented black beans

½   cup Shaoxing rice wine or sake

2   tablespoons sugar

2   large garlic cloves, finely grated

3   tablespoons finely grated fresh ginger

2   tablespoons vegetable oil

3   pounds pork shoulder (pork butt), cut into long 1-inch-thick strips

1. Put the black beans in a bowl and add water to cover. Soak for about 15 minutes to get rid of the excess salt. Drain and mince.

2. In another bowl, whisk together the rice wine and sugar until the sugar is completely dissolved. Add the black beans, garlic, ginger, and oil and stir until well combined.

3. Put the pork and marinade in a resealable gallon plastic bag. Squeezing out the air, seal the bag. Holding on to the ends, shake the bag to coat the pieces evenly with the marinade. Refrigerate the meat for 4 to 8 hours, turning the bag occasionally to redistribute the marinade.

4. Prepare a hot fire in a charcoal grill, or preheat a gas grill to 500°F (high). Grill the pork strips, turning the pieces frequently to prevent burning, 6 to 8 minutes for medium to medium-well. Transfer pork to a serving dish.

NOTE: If you prefer a smooth marinade, put the marinade ingredients in a mini food processor and process to a smooth consistency.

PORK PATTIES

Serves 6 to 8

1 tablespoon fish sauce

1 tablespoon sugar

1 tablespoon vegetable oil

1 small shallot, finely grated

1 small garlic clove, finely grated

1 lemongrass stalk, trimmed, peeled, and finely grated (white and light green parts)

Freshly ground black pepper to taste

2 pounds pork shoulder (pork butt), coarsely ground

Toasted Rice Flour (page 54) for coating

This pork patty recipe is perfect for making *banh mi,* a popular Vietnamese sandwich. Grill the pork patties and serve in a baguette or wrapped in Scallion Flat Breads (page 59) with the works: fresh lettuce leaves, sliced cucumber, and julienned carrots. Add some herbs such as mint, Thai basil, and cilantro. Dab the patties with Ginger–Garlic Chili Paste (page 50) for a spicy finish. Note that it is important to grind the pork coarsely—think Italian sausage consistency—so the meat stays juicy. Sweet and savory, with citrus flavor notes, these pork patties can also be served over rice with sweet and sour vegetables such as Pickled Daikon, Carrot, and Cucumber (page 76) or Spicy Cucumber and Red Onion Salad (page 85).

1. In a bowl, whisk together the fish sauce and sugar until the sugar is completely dissolved. Add the oil, shallot, garlic, lemongrass, pepper, and ground pork, and mix until well combined. Divide the pork mixture into 18 portions and shape each portion into round patties. Lightly roll each patty in the toasted rice flour to coat.

2. Prepare a medium-hot fire in a charcoal grill, or preheat a gas grill to 400°F (medium-high). Grill the patties, turning the pieces frequently to prevent burning, until crisp and medium-well done, about 10 minutes. Transfer pork patties to a serving dish.

LEMONGRASS AND KAFFIR LIME LEAF MARINATED PORK SKEWERS

Serves 6 to 8

The citrus and floral notes of the lemongrass and kaffir lime leaf marinade make this one of the most flavorful, light, and refreshing pork dishes you will ever eat. While the lemongrass is tasted at every bite, the kaffir lime leaf is a surprise note especially apparent at the finish. Palm sugar counterbalances the salty fish sauce base and adds a subtle coconut note. Serve these fragrant pork skewers with Sweet, Sour, and Spicy Fish Sauce Dressing (page 42) and Rice Vermicelli with Scallion Oil and Fresh Vegetables (page 71). The citrus and floral notes of this marinade are also especially well suited for seafood, such as eel, swordfish, shrimp, lobster, and squid.

¾ cup palm sugar or granulated sugar

¾ cup fish sauce

3 lemongrass stalks, trimmed, peeled, and finely grated (white and light green parts)

4 large garlic cloves, finely grated

4 large fresh kaffir lime leaves, minced

2 tablespoons vegetable oil

2 pounds pork tenderloin, cut into ⅛-inch-thick diagonal slices

18 long bamboo skewers

1. In a medium bowl, whisk together the sugar and fish sauce until the sugar is completely dissolved. Stir in the lemongrass, garlic, kaffir lime leaves, and oil until evenly distributed.

2. Put the pork and marinade in a resealable gallon plastic bag. Squeezing out the air, seal the bag. Holding on to the ends, shake the bag to coat the pieces evenly with the marinade. Refrigerate for 1 hour, turning the bag over every 15 minutes or so to redistribute the marinade.

3. Soak the bamboo skewers in water for 30 minutes. Meanwhile, prepare a hot fire in a charcoal grill, or preheat a gas grill to 500°F (high).

4. Thread the pork on the skewers, leaving about 1½ inches free on either end. Grill the pork skewers, turning them once, until golden, 1 to 2 minutes. Transfer pork to a serving dish.

SLOW-COOKED LEG OF LAMB

Serves about 12

One 8- to 12-pound leg of lamb,
bone-in or butterflied

¼ to ⅓ cup Spice Route Blend
(page 53)

2 tablespoons kosher salt

2 tablespoons sugar

1 tablespoon freshly ground
black pepper

A distant cousin of Kansas City smoked brisket, this recipe evolved from two other slow-cooked dishes: the first, a smoked lamb leg yielding meat that can easily be pulled apart with 2 forks, the second, lamb braised in its own juices and a bit of wine. I like to make this type of meal once every year or so, and it is a great way to cook if you are spending the day outside enjoying light activities and generally being available to check on the meat as it progresses. The paybacks are that the cookout will become a never-to-be-forgotten event, the dish will feed an army of guests, and the guests will be plenty hungry by dinner if they smell the dish cooking during the day. Though you can use a charcoal or gas grill, you might also want to invite more friends and use the fire-pit method, covering the meat with banana leaves to hold the flavors and infuse your lamb with a fruity back note. If you are going to bother digging the pit, you might as well invite a big group, get 2 legs of lamb, and add a few potatoes and some sweet corn.

1. Place the leg of lamb on a baking sheet. In a bowl, mix together the spice blend, salt, sugar, and pepper. Rub the dry spice blend all over the leg of lamb. Refrigerate the lamb on the baking sheet, uncovered, for at least 12 hours or overnight.

2. Prepare a low indirect fire in a charcoal grill (see page 34), or preheat a gas grill to 250°F (low). Place a rectangular drip pan in the center with the coals around it. Place the leg of lamb on the grill over the drip pan. Or, cook the lamb in a low-heat fire pit (see page 33). Cover the grill or pit, but leave the grill vents open a bit so that enough air can circulate to keep the fire going. Cook the lamb until fork-tender, 8 to 10 hours depending on the size of the leg and the exact temperature of the heat source. Check every 30 minutes to make sure the heat is still going but is not hot enough to burn the meat. You may need to adjust the fire, replenishing or removing some of the heat source as required to keep the temperature roughly at 250°F. Turn the leg every 2 hours.

3. Transfer the meat to a carving board and cut it crosswise, or if it is super-tender (falling off the bone), pull it apart with two forks to serve.

NOTE: Slow-cooking a large cut of meat on any grill can be challenging. The fire can flare up due to dripping fat, and you definitely need to maintain a steady low temperature, around 250°F to 270°F. If you are using a smoker-type barbecue with a built-in fire pit off to the side, put the charcoal in the fire pit and slow-cook the leg of lamb in the grilling/smoking chamber. Use a thermometer specifically designed for barbecues to check the fire temperature.

LAMB MARINATED IN YELLOW SPICE PASTE

Serves 6 to 8

Lamb can be an acquired taste. In particular, it has a strong flavor that many Asians find overwhelming. Some cultures would have you soak the meat in milk to moderate the flavor, or parboil the meat for 10 to 15 minutes prior to cooking it thoroughly. When it comes to grilling lamb, I like to marinate it in coconut milk. Not only does the coconut milk tame the strong flavor of lamb, it also helps to tenderize the meat. A yellow herbal paste gives the meat a beautiful yellow hue and lends the meat pungent herbal and spicy flavors. This recipe can turn lamb skeptics into lamb lovers. Serve with refreshing Cucumber and Preserved Lemon Yogurt (page 48). It is also perfect with Scallion Flat Breads (page 59), or any type of flat bread, such as Middle Eastern pitas or Indian–inspired Parathas (page 62).

¾ cup Yellow Spice Paste (page 52)

⅓ cup unsweetened coconut milk

2 to 3 pounds leg of lamb, cut into ¾-inch cubes

12 long bamboo skewers

1. In a bowl, stir together the yellow spice paste and coconut milk until well combined.

2. Put the meat and marinade in a resealable gallon plastic bag. Squeezing out the air, seal the bag. Holding on to the ends, shake the bag to coat the pieces evenly with the marinade. Refrigerate the meat for 4 to 6 hours, turning occasionally to redistribute the marinade.

3. Soak the bamboo skewers in water for 30 minutes. Meanwhile, prepare a hot fire in a charcoal grill, or preheat a gas grill to 500°F (high). Thread about 6 pieces of lamb on each skewer. Grill the lamb skewers, turning the pieces frequently to prevent burning, until crisp and medium to medium-rare, about 4 minutes. Transfer lamb to a serving dish.

SPICED YOGURT LAMB KEBOBS

Serves 6 to 8

Yogurt is used in the marinade for this lamb dish to tame the heat from the chilies and the pungent flavors of the spices. A drizzle or two of freshly squeezed citrus juice refreshes the palate. Serve with Minty Silken Tofu Dip (page 44), Pineapple and Onion Chutney (page 46), Fresh Tomato Chutney (page 47), and Parathas (page 62).

½ cup plain Greek yogurt

2 large shallots, finely grated

2 large garlic cloves, finely grated

1½ to 2 tablespoons finely grated fresh ginger

2 red Thai chilies, stemmed, seeded, and minced

1½ teapoons Spice Route Blend (page 53)

1 teaspoon kosher salt

3 pounds leg of lamb, cut into ¾-inch cubes

16 long bamboo skewers

2 lemons, each cut into 6 wedges

1. In a medium bowl, mix together the yogurt, shallots, garlic, ginger, and chilies until well blended. Add the spice blend and salt and stir until well combined. Set aside.

2. Put the lamb cubes and marinade in a resealable gallon plastic bag. Squeezing out the air, seal the bag. Holding on to the ends, shake the bag to coat the pieces evenly with the marinade. Refrigerate for 3 hours, turning the bag over every hour or so.

3. Soak the bamboo skewers in water for 30 minutes. Meanwhile prepare a hot fire in a charcoal grill, or preheat a gas grill to 500°F (high). Thread 4 to 5 lamb cubes on each skewer. Grill, turning the skewers frequently to prevent burning, about 5 minutes for medium to medium-rare. Transfer to a serving dish and garnish with the lemon wedges.

GARLIC-PEPPER MARINATED HANGER STEAK

Serves 6 to 8

⅓ cup mushroom soy sauce

⅓ cup sugar

10 large garlic cloves, finely grated

2 teaspoons freshly ground black pepper

1 tablespoon vegetable oil

2½ pounds hanger steak, cut into 8 equal pieces, each weighing about 5 ounces

One of the most delicious, inexpensive, and underrated cuts of beef is the humble hanger steak. Now gaining popularity in the United States, it has just the right lean-to-fat ratio, about 70 percent to 30 percent. (The hanger cut has long been a staple in French cooking, where it is considered to be among the most flavorful cuts of beef.) When you combine hanger steak with garlic and pepper, you have a grill dish made in heaven. The secret here is the marinade, which uses mushroom soy sauce. This Asian staple contains molasses and has a smoky character well suited for beef and strong-flavored specialty meats such as ostrich and buffalo. The net result is an extraordinarily tender and deeply flavored steak redolent with sweet, rich, smoky notes; when cooked medium-rare, the steak just about melts in your mouth. Serve thinly sliced and wrapped in Scallion Flat Breads (page 59) with Pineapple and Onion Chutney (page 46), or make beef rolls for an appetizer.

1. In a large bowl, whisk together the soy sauce and sugar until the sugar is completely dissolved. Stir in the garlic, pepper, and oil until well combined.

2. Place the hanger steaks and marinade in a resealable gallon plastic bag. Squeezing out the air, seal the bag. Holding on to the ends, shake the bag to coat the pieces evenly with the marinade. Refrigerate for 4 hours, turning the bag over every 30 minutes or so to redistribute the marinade.

3. Prepare a hot fire in a charcoal grill, or preheat a gas grill to 500°F (high). Grill the hanger steaks, turning them frequently to prevent burning, until crisp and medium-rare, 6 to 8 minutes. Transfer steak to a serving dish.

GRILLED BEEF IN GRAPE LEAVES

Serves 6 to 8

Wrapped in grape leaves, ground sirloin retains its sweet juiciness. Mildly spiced with shallot and garlic, with lemongrass overtones, these skewered grape leaf rolls make great finger food. Grape leaves are sold in brine, generally packaged in glass jars, and are located in the International section of many markets. Serve with steamed rice and Asian Coleslaw (page 77).

1   pound ground sirloin beef

1   large shallot, minced

1   large garlic clove, minced

1   lemongrass stalk, trimmed, peeled, and finely grated (white and light green parts)

1   tablespoon sugar

1   tablespoon fish sauce

16   long bamboo skewers

32   grape leaves in brine

Vegetable oil for brushing

Sweet, Sour, and Spicy Fish Sauce Dressing (page 42) for dipping

1. In a large bowl, combine the beef, shallot, garlic, lemongrass, sugar, and fish sauce. Stir until well blended. Cover and refrigerate for 1 hour.

2. Soak the bamboo skewers in water for 30 minutes. Meanwhile prepare a hot fire in a charcoal grill, or preheat a gas grill to 500°F (high).

3. Soak the grape leaves in several changes of water to get rid of the brine flavor. Divide the beef mixture into 32 equal portions (about 1 tablespoon per portion). Place a grape leaf flat (widest side closest to you) on a double layer of paper towels to drain. Shape one meat mixture into a 1½-inch-long sausage and place it horizontally across the wide end of the leaf. Fold the wide end over the filling once. Fold the sides in and roll up as you would a spring roll, enclosing the meat. The roll should be compact and fairly tight. Repeat to make 32 rolls.

4. Thread 4 grape leaf rolls on 2 parallel skewers. Repeat with the remaining skewers and rolls. Brush each roll with vegetable oil and grill the rolls, flipping them every 15 seconds or so, until crisp and cooked through, 3 to 4 minutes. Serve with the dipping sauce.

GRILLED BARELY MARINATED BEEF

Serves 6 to 8

This recipe is a perfect example of how a few simple ingredients can create bold, complex flavoring. The sweet, salty, and herbal overtones are unexpected when you eat this marinated marbled beef. If you are a fan of Korean barbecue, in which raw beef is cooked by diners on a built-in hibachi at the center of the table, you will recognize this dish. You can cook the beef on your outdoor grill instead, and bring it to the table with tender Boston lettuce leaves for wrapping and dipping in two complementary sauces for a tangy, sweet, and spicy finish. The key to this wonderful grilled beef is the cut of meat. It should be marbled, or at least 30 percent fat. Premium buttery cuts like rib eye and sirloin are perfect. A less expensive yet delicious substitute is chuck, but be sure to select marbled chuck. Korean and Japanese markets offer meats, including beef, pork, and chicken, already sliced thin. These are so perfectly cut that they are hard to pass up. If you do not have that option, simply freeze the meat for 30 to 45 minutes for easy slicing. The slices should be no more than 1/16 of an inch thick. Serve with Sushi Rice in Fried Tofu Pockets (page 64) and baby greens tossed in Miso Salad Dressing (page 39).

¼ cup thin soy sauce

3 tablespoons sugar

1 tablespoon vegetable oil

1 teaspoon dark sesame oil

1 teaspoon sesame seeds, toasted (see page 25)

3 garlic cloves, grated

3 scallions, trimmed and minced (white and green parts)

2 pounds marbled beef sirloin, rib eye, or chuck, sliced paper-thin against the grain

Spicy Vinegar Dipping Sauce (page 43) for dipping

Sweet and Sour Chili and Bean Paste (page 49) for dipping

1. Prepare a hot fire in a charcoal grill, or preheat a gas grill to 500°F (high).

2. In a large bowl, whisk together the soy sauce and sugar until the sugar is completely dissolved. Stir in the vegetable and sesame oils, sesame seeds, garlic, and scallions until well combined. Add the beef, tossing it with your hands to make sure it is evenly coated on all sides. Cover the bowl and allow the meat to marinate for about 15 minutes.

3. Pick up a few slices of beef at a time with kitchen tongs and place them on the grill. There is no need to separate each slice. The bunched-up meat will ensure an equal amount of cooked, medium-rare, and crisp parts, allowing for a variety of textures in a single bite. Grill the beef slices, turning them every 5 seconds or so, until crisp, 1 to 2 minutes. Serve with the dipping sauces.

BEEF FILET MIGNON CUBES WITH SWEET LIME DIPPING SAUCE

Serves 6 to 8

Inspired by a Cambodian dish called *sach kho loc lac,* which I first tasted at the Hotel le Royal in Phnom Penh, this recipe has a range of flavors not quickly forgotten. Cubed filet mignon is marinated in a mushroom soy sauce and thick soy marinade and sweetened with sugar. When the beef is grilled, the resulting flavors are reminiscent of smoky licorice. The tender meat cubes are then dipped in a generously portioned sour lime and spicy black pepper sauce. Serve over rice with lettuce leaves for wrapping the beef, or serve with Asian Coleslaw (page 77).

2   tablespoons mushroom soy sauce

¼   teaspoon thick soy sauce

2   tablespoons plus ¼ cup sugar

1   tablespoon vegetable oil

2   pounds filet mignon, cut into ¾-inch cubes

1   cup fresh lime juice

2   teaspoons freshly ground black pepper

1   teaspoon kosher salt

18   long bamboo skewers

1. In a small bowl, whisk together the mushroom soy sauce, dark soy sauce, and the 2 tablespoons sugar until the sugar is completely dissolved. Whisk in the oil.

2. Put the cubed meat and marinade into a resealable gallon plastic bag. Squeezing out the air, seal the bag. Holding on to the ends, shake the bag to coat the pieces evenly. Marinate for 30 minutes.

3. In a bowl, whisk together the lime juice, ¼ cup sugar, pepper, and salt until the sugar is completely dissolved. Set the dipping sauce aside.

4. Soak the bamboo skewers in water for 30 minutes. Meanwhile prepare a hot fire in a charcoal grill, or preheat a gas grill to 500°F (high). Thread about 6 cubes of meat on each skewer. Grill the skewered meat, turning frequently to prevent burning, until crisp and medium-rare, about 2 minutes. Serve with the lime dipping sauce on the side.

MISO-MARINATED SIRLOIN

Serves 6 to 8

In this dish, inspired by Hiroko Shimbo, a well–known Japanese chef and author, red miso paste is used to marinate a sirloin steak. The fragrant leafy herb known as shiso, or perilla leaf, adds a mild mustardlike spicy note that is particularly well suited to beef. While the marinade is bold, it transforms itself when the meat is grilled, becoming subtle, with sweet, salty, and nutty flavor notes. This dish is wonderful served with fresh leafy greens, or with Grilled Vegetables (page 93) tossed in Miso Salad Dressing (page 39).

½ cup aka-miso (red miso)

⅓ cup mirin (sweet sake)

1 tablespoon sugar

1 garlic clove, finely grated

1 tablespoon vegetable oil

1 tablespoon sake

8 fresh shiso leaves, minced

3 pounds 1-inch-thick sirloin steak, cut into 8 pieces

1. In a small bowl, whisk together the aka-miso, mirin, and sugar until smooth. Stir in the garlic, oil, sake, and shiso.

2. Put the meat and marinade in a resealable gallon plastic bag. Squeezing out the air, seal the bag. Holding on to the ends, shake the bag to coat the pieces evenly with the marinade. Refrigerate for at least 6 or up to 24 hours, turning the bag every hour or so to redistribute the marinade.

3. Prepare a hot fire in a charcoal grill, or preheat a gas grill to 500°F (high). Grill the steaks about 7 minutes for medium-rare, turning once. Transfer steaks to a serving dish.

TERIYAKI VENISON

Serves 6 to 8

Teriyaki is a popular Japanese sauce, one Americanized enough at this point to show up on various fast-food restaurant menus as a heavy-handed sugar and soy sauce concoction. The name derives from the Japanese *teri,* meaning "gloss," and *yaki,* meaning "broiled," and the sweet mirin-based soy sauce may be used as a marinade or drizzled over any number of grilled fish or meat dishes. In this recipe, the teriyaki is both a marinade and a finishing sauce.

1 cup mirin (sweet sake)

½ cup thin soy sauce

¼ cup tamari

1 cup sake

¼ cup thinly sliced fresh ginger

5 scallions, trimmed and lightly crushed (white and green parts)

3 large garlic cloves, crushed

1 tablespoon tapioca starch mixed with 2 tablespoons spring or filtered water

2 pounds boneless venison, cut into ¾-inch cubes

18 long bamboo skewers

1. In a small saucepan, bring the mirin, soy sauce, tamari, and sake to a gentle boil over medium heat. Reduce the heat to low and add the ginger, scallions, and garlic. Simmer until reduced to 2 cups, about 30 minutes. Gradually stir the tapioca starch mixture into the sauce. While stirring, continue to simmer until slightly thickened, about 3 minutes. Strain the sauce, let cool to room temperature, and transfer to a container. Store in the refrigerator for up to 2 weeks.

2. Put the cubed meat and half the marinade (reserving the rest for drizzling) into a resealable gallon plastic bag. Squeezing out the air, seal the bag. Holding on to the ends, shake the bag to coat the pieces evenly. Marinate for 30 minutes.

3. Soak the bamboo skewers in water for 30 minutes. Meanwhile, prepare a hot fire in a charcoal grill, or preheat a gas grill to 500°F (high). Thread about 6 cubes of meat on each skewer. Grill the skewered meat, turning frequently to prevent burning, until crisp and medium-rare, about 2 minutes. Serve the skewered venison drizzled with some of the reserved teriyaki sauce.

CHAPTER 8 | SWEETS AND DRINKS

"My father told me that Asians eat their dessert first."

I stared at my husband in disbelief. "He used to spend time in Chinatown in Boston," my husband went on, "and somehow he got the idea that sweets were taken as part of the meal."

"You Irish and your stories," I said, ready to dismiss the idea out of hand. But he insisted. "He must have seen something to make that observation. He was telling me about something he had actually experienced. What could it have been?"

"Wait," I said. "He was not all wrong. Asian savory main dishes often include either sugar, palm sugar, or honey to counterbalance the salty soy sauce, fish sauce, or shrimp paste seasonings, for example. And they traditionally eat fresh fruits—often tart citrus fruit—at the end of their meals."

"Go on," my husband said, with a gleam in his eye.

"And," I was thinking out loud now, "because the entire meal often has sweet elements throughout, it would be redundant to serve sweet ice cream, pastry, crêpes, or puddings at the end of the meal. You need a palate cleanser at the end, something acid. Those sweets are more likely to be had as an afternoon snack with tea, and the tea is never sweetened because the foods are already sweet."

My husband smiled. His dad had been redeemed.

Fresh citrus fruits are the preferred "dessert" in many Asian cuisines because their acid content aids in digestion, and because the flavors are refreshing. We can't always (if ever) get the wonderful array of fresh Asian fruits widely available in their markets, but we can get a sense of them. Citrus Fruit Salad with Asian Herb Broth (page 154) is a good example. A take on classic Asian fruit platters, it consists of sections of lemons, limes, oranges, and grapefruit segments served in a sweetened herbal broth—all lightly chilled. Light and refreshing, it makes for a wonderful presentation.

With the internationalization of travel and adoption of Western customs in the East, sweet desserts are now commonly available there. In this chapter, I include a number of desserts perfectly attuned to a grilled meal or to serve as an afternoon snack with tea. And the Grilled Fruit medley (page 91) in the vegetables and fruits chapter can be served either as a side dish or a dessert.

In the same "creative sweets for dessert" vein, I also include a few classic Asian coconut dishes. Try tapioca pudding with grilled corn and banana, for example. It can be served hot, at room temperature, or chilled—a real treat on hot summer days. Toasted Coconut Ice Cream (page 148) was an instant favorite at my table, and is apt to become one at yours, too. Rich with coconut flavor, it is surprisingly light on the palate, and has a crunch from the toasted shredded coconut incorporated into the ice cream. A simple-to-make coconut sticky rice with freshly sliced sweet mango is included, too, a variation on the popular Thai dessert. There is also Herb Ice Pops with Fresh Berries with a kind of frozen herbal tea infusion, good for digestion and refreshing, wonderfully colorful.

Summer grills are great for experimenting with all sorts of cool drinks, with or without alcohol. I include some classics here, but with an exotic fruit twist. Try my version of a mint julep, Watermelon Julep (page 158). Litchi Margarita (page 157) has the kick of the original, but lends the classic an exotic floral note. The Kiwi Rum Cocktail (page 157) is refreshing and sweet, with a sour note.

Nonalcoholic drinks include Cucumber Lemonade (page 160), based on an iced sliced lemon and cucumber spa drink I was served in Calistoga. It is terrific unsweetened and chilled, but if you have a sweet tooth, try adding simple syrup (see note, page 160) or agave syrup (available in natural foods or specialty stores) for a subtly sweet note.

Drunk in South America for hundreds of years, yerba maté is a caffeine-free leaf tea with an intense smoky flavor. Soy milk and honey give it an Asian flair, taming the pungent, bitter note. My husband likes to joke that it is such a great mood lifter and energizer that it should be illegal in a few states.

HERB ICE POPS WITH FRESH BERRIES

Serves 6 to 8

This refreshing and pungent chilled dessert makes for a fun presentation at any summer table. You can use one type of berry, or a mixture. Herbs and rhizomes add exotic notes and aid digestion. The citrus juice balances the sweetness and lifts the flavor notes.

4   cups spring or filtered water

4   kaffir lime leaves, bruised

¼   cup thinly sliced fresh ginger

¼   cup thinly sliced fresh galangal

10 fresh Thai basil leaves, bruised

2   lemongrass stalks, trimmed, peeled, and thinly sliced on the diagonal (white and light green parts)

    Juice of 1 lime or lemon

1   cup sugar

    Pinch of kosher salt

1   cup fresh berries, such as raspberries, strawberries, and blueberries

1. In a large saucepan, combine the water, kaffir lime leaves, ginger, galangal, Thai basil, lemongrass, lime or lemon juice, sugar, and salt. Bring to a boil over high heat. Lower the heat to medium and continue to gently boil until reduced to about 3 cups and thickened to a light syrup consistency, about 30 minutes. Strain to remove the solids and refrigerate the infusion for at least 12 hours or overnight.

2. Mix the berries with the herb-infused liquid. Pour into popsicle containers and freeze overnight before serving.

TOASTED COCONUT ICE CREAM

Makes about 1 quart

Coconut is widely used in Asian cookery, appearing in both sweet and savory foods. I especially like its refreshing notes during the summer, and its rich flavor blends exceptionally well with slightly more acidic fruit flavors. This ice cream celebrates the coconut in all its glory, from its creamy milk to its wonderfully crunchy texture. Neither too light nor too heavy, this is just about the perfect dessert or snack for a hot summer day. Grated toasted coconut is incorporated into this ice cream. To counterbalance the ice cream's sweet character, a small amount of salt is added, as is a lemongrass note, both of which are just noticeable on the finish.

2   cups unsweetened shredded fresh coconut

3   cups plus 2 tablespoons unsweetened coconut milk

1   cup half-and-half

3   lemongrass stalks, trimmed, peeled, halved crosswise, and crushed (white and light green parts)

¼   teaspoon kosher salt

4   large egg yolks

¾   cup sugar

1   tablespoon tapioca starch

1. In a dry skillet, toast the coconut over medium heat, stirring constantly, until rich golden, about 5 minutes. Transfer to a dish and let cool. Store in a dark, cool place until ready to use.

2. Fill a medium saucepan half-full with water. Bring to a boil over high heat. Reduce the heat to medium. In a medium stainless-steel bowl, combine the 3 cups coconut milk, the half-and-half, lemongrass stalks, and salt and stir well. Place the bowl containing the coconut milk mixture on top of the saucepan of simmering water, and simmer for 30 minutes.

3. Meanwhile, in another medium stainless-steel bowl, whisk together the egg yolks and sugar until pale and thick. Gradually whisk half of the hot coconut milk mixture into the cold egg mixture. Gradually whisk this mixture into the remaining coconut milk set over the saucepan of simmering water. Whisk constantly until thickened and velvety, about 20 minutes.

4. In a small bowl, mix the tapioca starch with the 2 tablespoons coconut milk and add it to the coconut milk mixture set over the saucepan. Continue whisking to a custard consistency, about 5 minutes more. (The mixture should coat the back of a spoon.) Pass the custard through a fine-mesh sieve set over a heat-proof bowl, place in an ice bath and let cool. Press a layer of plastic wrap directly onto the surface of the custard and refrigerate overnight.

5. The next day, pour the custard into an ice cream maker and freeze according to the manufacturer's instructions. Halfway through processing the ice cream, while it is still soft, add about ⅓ cup of the toasted coconut. Transfer the ice cream to a container and place in the freezer until ready to serve. Garnish each serving with some of the remaining toasted coconut.

SWEET COCONUT TAPIOCA WITH SUMMER CORN AND BANANA

Makes about 2 quarts

Coconut tapioca is popular in many parts of Asia, and it ranges from soupy to thick in consistency, with variations in between. Corn—a cereal—lends itself well to the tapioca mix, and I like to use it in creative ways during its peak late-summer season. The crunchy corn is especially nice with sweet and tender Asian bananas when both are grilled until lightly caramelized. These two garnishes are a great pairing, but you can also use other grilled fruits or tubers, including pineapple, mangos, peaches, sweet potatoes, or yams.

Two 13½-ounce cans unsweetened coconut milk

3½ cups spring or filtered water

⅓ cup palm sugar or granulated sugar

½ teaspoon kosher salt

½ cup small-pearl tapioca

1½ cups grilled yellow or sugar-butter corn kernels (page 93)

4 Asian or 2 regular bananas, grilled (see note, page 91)

Toasted sesame seeds for garnish (see page 25)

In a large saucepan, bring the coconut milk, water, sugar, and salt to a boil over medium-high heat. Reduce the heat to medium-low and, stirring constantly, add the tapioca pearls in a slow and steady stream. Cook, stirring occasionally, until the tapioca is transparent, about 40 minutes. Serve warm, at room temperature, or chilled, garnished with grilled corn, bananas, and toasted sesame seeds.

Variation

If you would rather not grill the corn and bananas, simply steam 2 to 3 ears of corn and slice the kernels off the cobs. The bananas can be peeled and diced fresh (be sure to use ripe ones). Add the bananas to the tapioca while it is still hot and immediately after you have turned off the heat. Cover and let the bananas steam in the tapioca, for about 15 minutes. Serve hot or chilled.

COCONUT STICKY RICE WITH MANGO

Serves 6 to 8

Sweet and savory, this coconut sticky rice makes for a wonderful dessert when paired with fresh mangos. Be sure to use yellow, ripe kidney-shaped mangos if at all possible. They are the sweetest and least fibrous of the mangos available. Sold in Asian markets or by street vendors in some Chinatowns, they are well worth the effort it takes to get them. Unfortunately, the mangos most commonly sold in Western markets tend to be green to yellowish-orange in color, double in size, rounder in shape, and too fibrous and sour to really enjoy as a sweet dessert. In a pinch, you can also make this delicious sweet coconut sticky rice with ripe pineapple. Minus the fruit, this sticky rice dish also complements all sorts of grilled, braised, and stir-fried dishes.

2   cups sticky white rice

4   cups plus 1½ tablespoons tap water

2½ cups unsweetened coconut milk

1½ cups spring or filtered water

¼   cup sugar

½   teaspoon salt

1½ tablespoons tapioca starch

2   small to medium yellow kidney-shaped mangos, peeled, pitted, and thinly sliced

    Toasted sesame seeds for garnish (see page 25)

1. In a large bowl, soak the sticky rice in the 4 cups tap water until the grains absorb most of the water, about 4 hours. Drain.

2. Place a steamer rack on top of a wok filled half-full with water. Line the rack with a double layer of cheesecloth and spread the soaked rice on top in an even layer. Pull up the cheesecloth on the sides to enclose the rice. Place a lid on top and steam over high heat until the rice is translucent, about 25 minutes.

3. Meanwhile, in a medium saucepan, combine the coconut milk with the 1½ cups spring water and bring to a gentle boil over medium heat. Stir in the sugar and salt.

4. In a cup, mix the tapioca starch with the 1½ tablespoons tap water. Gradually stir the starch mixture into the coconut sauce. Continue to cook until the sauce is lightly thickened, about 5 minutes. Remove the sauce from the heat.

5. Transfer the sticky rice to a bowl, removing the cheesecloth. While the rice is still hot, stir in 2 cups of the coconut sauce until the rice has absorbed it all. (At this time, you can serve this coconut-flavored rice at room temperature with savory foods. As part of a main course, this recipe serves 4.)

6. To serve, divide the rice among 6 plates and top with some sliced mango. Drizzle each serving with some of the remaining coconut sauce and sprinkle lightly with toasted sesame seeds. Serve at room temperature.

CITRUS FRUIT SALAD WITH ASIAN HERB BROTH

Serves 6 to 8

A blend of refreshing citrus fruits and pungent herbs, this salad in an herbal broth can be a pleasantly surprising and palate-lifting finale to any meal, especially when grilled meats have been served. Grapefruit (pink or yellow), lemons, oranges, and limes are generally available year-round in Western markets, as is mint, and you can work with these solely if you have to. Blood oranges and Meyer lemons are usually available in winter, and they make a wonderful addition.

4   cups spring or filtered water

4   fresh kaffir lime leaves, bruised

¼   cup thinly sliced fresh ginger

¼   cup thinly sliced fresh galangal

10   fresh Thai basil leaves, bruised

2   lemongrass stalks, trimmed, peeled, and thinly sliced on the diagonal (white and light green parts)

⅓   cup sugar

Pinch of kosher salt

2   pink grapefruits

2   lemons

2   oranges

2   limes

12   fresh mint leaves for garnish

1. In a saucepan, combine the 4 cups water, kaffir lime leaves, ginger, galangal, Thai basil, lemongrass, sugar, and salt. Bring to a boil over high heat, then reduce the heat to low and simmer until reduced to about 1 cup, 10 to 15 minutes. Strain, discard the solids, and refrigerate the broth until chilled.

2. Peel and segment the fruit (see note, page 45).

3. Distribute the citrus segments among 6 dessert bowls. Pour an equal amount of broth over each serving of fruit, garnish with the mint leaves, and serve.

YERBA MATÉ SOY DRINK

Makes about 4 cups

Yerba maté is a South American infusion that dates back hundreds of years. It energizes without the ill effects of caffeine. The smoky flavor of the leaves, which come from ilex trees deep in the Amazon forest, is pungent, like fermented tea. I like to add unsweetened soy milk (an Asian staple) and honey to the mix for a mild but still flavorful sweet drink. Look for unsweetened soy milk. Presweetened ones will make the drink cloyingly sweet while denying it its rich honey–flavored note. This drink is delicious chilled.

⅓ cup loose yerba maté

2¼ cups spring or filtered water

2 cups unsweetened soy milk

¼ cup honey

1. Put the yerba maté in a French press coffeemaker. In a saucepan, bring the water just to a boil over high heat. Turn the heat off and pour just enough of the water into the French press to moisten the leaves and release their essence. Pour the remaining water into the French press. Stir the contents. The leaves will float on the top and slowly work their way back to the bottom. Once the leaves have settled to the bottom, place the lid on top of the French press and push the stem down to press the leaves.

2. Pour the soy milk and honey into a large pitcher or glass bottle. Add the yerba maté infusion and stir to mix thoroughly and melt the honey. If using a bottle, seal and shake. Refrigerate for at least 6 hours.

KIWI RUM COCKTAIL

Serves 1

This cocktail is wonderful in summer. Refreshingly sweet and sour, the color is beautiful whether you select green or golden (yellow) kiwis. Bear in mind that golden kiwis tend to be sweeter than the green types, so you may want to adjust the amount of syrup accordingly.

1½ ounces white rum

1 ounce green or golden kiwi juice (see note)

1 ounce fresh lime juice

1 ounce simple syrup (see note, page 160)

1 cup ice cubes

Lime twist for garnish (optional)

In a cocktail shaker, combine the rum, kiwi juice, lime juice, simple syrup, and ice cubes. Close the shaker and shake a few times. Pour the cocktail, holding back the ice, into a martini glass. Garnish with a lime twist, if desired.

NOTE: To juice a kiwi, peel and chop 1 kiwifruit. Put it in a fine-mesh sieve set over a bowl. With the back of a large spoon, crush the kiwi pieces against the side of the sieve to release the juice. Discard the pulp and seeds.

LITCHI MARGARITA

Serves 1

Everyone seems to love the floral flavor of litchis. I've experimented with a number of litchi syrup cocktails, and they have been consistently popular with my guests. I combine litchi syrup with vodka (2 parts to 1, respectively), for example, for a simple but sweetish drink. I have also mixed it with Champagne (1 part to 3) for a quick, bubbly cocktail. Here, however, I offer a more complex drink, based on the classic margarita. Shaken not stirred (apologies to the martini), it combines the slight bitterness of tequila with the sweet fruit-noted smoothness of litchi, and it is always a hit.

Lime wedge and fine salt for garnish (optional)

2 ounces litchi syrup (from canned litchis)

1½ ounces tequila

1 ounce Triple Sec

1 ounce fresh lime juice

1 cup ice cubes

1. If you like, take the wedge of lime and run the pulp side over the rim of the glass. Scatter an even layer of salt in a dish wider than the rim of the glass. Put the rim of the glass down into the salt and lift.

2. In a cocktail shaker, combine the litchi syrup, tequila, Triple Sec, lime juice, and ice cubes. Close the shaker and shake a few times. Pour the cocktail, holding back the ice, into a salted or unsalted martini glass.

WATERMELON JULEP

Serves 1

This watermelon julep is based on the Southern mint julep, also known as the official drink of the Kentucky Derby. The classic is a concoction of bourbon flavored with crushed fresh mint leaves, sweetened with a bit of sugar, and cooled with ice. This version celebrates one of summer's best fruits, the watermelon, adding it to the mix. This is a "light" julep (when it comes to alcohol content), but feel free to experiment and make it to your liking. I enjoy the foreground flavor of sweet watermelon here, with bourbon on the finish. Fresh mint leaves are used as a garnish as an homage to the classic drink. For a variation, crush the leaves and steep them in the watermelon juice for 30 minutes prior to adding the bourbon.

2   ounces watermelon juice
    (see note)

1   ounce bourbon

2 to 4 ice cubes

1   fresh mint sprig for garnish

In a cocktail shaker, combine the watermelon juice and bourbon. Close the shaker and shake a few times. Pour the cocktail into a 6-ounce tumbler containing the ice cubes. Garnish with the mint.

NOTES: To juice a watermelon, put ¼ cup chopped watermelon into a fine-mesh sieve. Using the back of a large spoon, press it through twice.

To make a large batch of watermelon juleps, mix 16 ounces of watermelon juice (1½ cups to 2 cups chopped watermelon) with 8 ounces of bourbon and refrigerate until ready to serve.

CUCUMBER LEMONADE

Makes 4 cups

I got the idea for this unusual and refreshing cucumber lemonade on a trip to the Napa Valley one year. The original was an antioxidant drink made with water, cucumber, and lemon slices, and it was so delicious that I have been making it at home ever since. Rather than sliced ingredients, however, I use juice. The lemonade is particularly simple to make at the same time as preparing Cucumber and Preserved Lemon Yogurt (page 48), because cucumber juice is a by-product of that recipe. While this is unsweetened lemonade, you can add simple syrup or agave syrup (available in natural foods or specialty stores) to taste.

2   English (hothouse) cucumbers

½   cup fresh lemon juice

2½ cups spring or filtered water

    Simple Syrup (see note),
    to taste (optional)

1. Finely grate the cucumbers into a fine-mesh sieve set over a bowl. Drain the cucumber for 1 hour and collect the juices. (Reserve the pulp for Cucumber and Preserved Lemon Yogurt). Add the lemon juice and water, stir, and refrigerate until ready to use. Sweeten with simple syrup, if you like.

2. Alternatively, skip the spring water and simply fill an ice cube tray with the mixed cucumber and lemon juices and freeze. Add a couple of these ice cubes to a glass filled with sparkling water for each serving.

NOTE: To make simple syrup, in a medium saucepan, add 2 cups water to 1 cup sugar and gently boil over medium heat until reduced to a slightly thick syrup. Transfer to a jar, cover, and refrigerate for up to 6 months. Makes 1¼ cups.

SAMPLE MENUS

These sample grill menus incorporate recipes from all over Asia, and will allow you to share wonderful flavors and ingredients from China, Japan, Korea, Indonesia, Vietnam, Cambodia, and India with your family and friends. Each menu offers a well-balanced meal.

With regards to beverages, you can substitute nonalcoholic drinks for alcoholic drinks or vice versa. If you are drinking beer and wine with your meals (rather than or in addition to my cocktail and mixed-drink suggestions), note that spicy Asian-inspired foods do best with the blond beers typical of Asian breweries. If you want to go with European or American brands, stick to the light ales or lagers, and similar brews. Avoid very heavy dark or sweet beers, lagers, wheat, or fruit beers. Chinese, Japanese, Korean, Indonesian, Vietnamese, Cambodian, and Indian beers, among others, are often excellent. Indian pale ales also work with Indian-inspired foods. The Internet and other sources also offer Asian beers.

Light, young red wines such as the French Loire's Morgon or Chinon can be served lightly chilled. Brisk whites such as Sauvignon Blancs or lightly sweet Gewürztraminers are often your best choices for spicy grilled foods. Bubbly wines are good, too. Big, overly complex wines will be overwhelmed by the spicy notes.

Litchi Margarita
Spicy Sweet Soy Sauce Marinated Chicken
Sushi Rice in Fried Tofu Pockets
Baby Salad Greens with Miso
    Salad Dressing

Cucumber Lemonade
Garlic-Pepper Marinated
    Hanger Steak
Spicy Cucumber and Red Onion Salad
Pineapple and Onion Chutney
Parathas

Sweet Miso-Marinated Fish
Lemon-and-Ginger-Infused Soy Sauce
Sweet Summer Corn and Edamame Salad
    with Walnut-Miso Dressing
Green Tea and Plum Soba Medley
Sweet Coconut Tapioca with Summer Corn
    and Banana

Spicy Thai Basil and Lime Marinated
    Jumbo Shrimp
Rice Vermicelli with Scallion Oil and
    Fresh Vegetables
Sweet, Sour, and Spicy Fish Sauce Dressing

Kiwi Rum Cocktail
Slow-Cooked Leg of Lamb
Fresh Tomato Chutney
Smoky Eggplant Caviar
Sunchokes Braised in Sake
Parathas
Citrus Fruit Salad with Asian Herb Broth

Yerba Maté Soy Drink
Grilled Tofu with Ginger-Soy Dressing
Grilled Vegetables
Miso Salad Dressing
Toasted Coconut Ice Cream

Lemongrass and Kaffir Lime
    Leaf Marinated Pork Skewers
Spicy Peanut Sauce
Asian Coleslaw
Herbal Sticky Rice in Bamboo Leaves

Teriyaki Venison
Scallion Flat Breads
Grilled Baby Eggplants with Sweet
    Ginger-Miso Paste
Herb Ice Pops with Fresh Berries

Five-Spice Marinated Duck
Sour Mango Salad
Delicate Sesame Wraps

Watermelon Julep
Asian Clambake
Herbal Sticky Rice in Bamboo Leaves
Pickled Daikon, Carrot, and Cucumber,
Grilled Fruit

SOURCES

Following are sources for hard-to-find ingredients used in this book.

Diamond Organics
Highway 1
Moss Landing, CA 95039
Tel: (888) ORGANIC (674-2642)
Fax: (888) 888-6777
E-mail: info@diamondorganics.com
Web site: www.diamondorganics.com
Asian herbs and vegetables.

Melissa's/World Variety Produce Inc.
P.O. Box 21127
Los Angeles, CA 90021
Tel: (800) 588-0151
E-mail: hotline@melissas.com
Web site: www.melissas.com
Asian herbs and vegetables.

Penzeys Spices
Tel: (800) 741-7787
Fax: (262) 785-7678
Web site: www.penzeys.com
Dried spices.

Kalustyan's
c/o Marhaba International Inc.
123 Lexington Avenue
New York, NY 10016
Tel: (800) 352-3451 or (212) 685-3451
Fax: (212)-683-8458
E-mail: sales@kalustyans.com
Web site: www.kalustyans.com
Dried spices.

Importfood.com
P.O. Box 2054
Issaquah, WA 98027
Tel: (888) 618-THAI (8424) or (425) 687-1708
Fax: (425) 687-8413
E-mail: info@importfood.com
Web site: www.importfood.com
Asian condiments and herbs.

D'Artagnan
280 Wilson Avenue
Newark, NJ 07105
Tel: (800) 327-8246
Fax: (973) 465-1870
E-mail: orders@dartagnan.com
Web site: www.dartagnan.com
Specialty meats.

Uwajimaya
600 Fifth Avenue South, Suite 100
Seattle, WA 98104
Tel: (800) 889-1928 or (206) 624-6248
Web site: www.uwajimaya.com
Asian condiments, vegetables, and herbs.

Weber-Stephen Products Co.
200 East Daniels Road
Palatine, IL 60067
Tel: 1(800) 446-1071
Web site: www.weber.com
Charcoal and gas grills, and grilling tools.

INDEX

TABLE OF EQUIVALENTS

The exact equivalents in the following table have been rounded for convenience.

LIQUID/DRY MEASURES

U.S.	Metric
¼ teaspoon	1.25 milliliters
½ teaspoon	2.5 milliliters
1 teaspoon	5 milliliters
1 tablespoon (3 teaspoons)	15 milliliters
1 fluid ounce (2 tablespoons)	30 milliliters
¼ cup	60 milliliters
⅓ cup	80 milliliters
½ cup	120 milliliters
1 cup	240 milliliters
1 pint (2 cups)	480 milliliters
1 quart (4 cups, 32 ounces)	960 milliliters
1 gallon (4 quarts)	3.84 liters
1 ounce (by weight)	28 grams
1 pound	454 grams
2.2 pounds	1 kilogram

OVEN TEMPERATURE

Fahrenheit	Celsius	Gas
250	120	½
275	140	1
300	150	2
325	160	3
350	180	4
375	190	5
400	200	6
425	220	7
450	230	8
475	240	9
500	260	10

LENGTH

U.S.	Metric
1/16 inch	3 millimeters
¼ inch	6 millimeters
½ inch	12 millimeters
1 inch	2.5 centimeters